OUR MONEY
OUR SELVES

OUR MONEY OUR SELVES

MONEY MANAGEMENT FOR EACH STAGE OF A WOMAN'S LIFE

GINITA WALL, C.P.A., C.F.P.,
and the Editors of Consumer Reports Books

CONSUMER REPORTS BOOKS
A DIVISION OF CONSUMERS UNION
YONKERS, NEW YORK

Copyright © 1992 by Ginita Wall

Published by Consumers Union of United States, Inc.,
Yonkers, New York 10703.

Library of Congress Cataloging-in-Publication Data

Wall, Ginita.
    Our money, our selves : money management for each stage of a woman's life
by Ginita Wall and the editors of Consumer Reports Books.
        p.   cm.
    Includes bibliographical references and index.
    ISBN 0-89043-434-4
    1. Women—Finance, Personal.   2. Widows—Finance, Personal.
3. Divorced women—Finance, Personal.   I. Consumers Union of United
States.   II. Title.
HG179.W314   1992
332.024'042—dc20   91-48357
                                                                                       CIP

First printing, May 1992

Manufactured in the United States of America

Our Money, Our Selves is a Consumer Reports Book published by Consumers Union, the nonprofit organization that publishes *Consumer Reports,* the monthly magazine of test reports, product Ratings, and buying guidance. Established in 1936, Consumers Union is chartered under the Not-for-Profit Corporation Law of the State of New York.

The purposes of Consumers Union, as stated in its charter, are to provide consumers with information and counsel on consumer goods and services, to give information on all matters relating to the expenditure of the family income, and to initiate and to cooperate with individual and group efforts seeking to create and maintain decent living standards.

Consumers Union derives its income solely from the sale of *Consumer Reports* and other publications. In addition, expenses of occasional public service efforts may be met, in part, by nonrestrictive, noncommercial contributions, grants, and fees. Consumers Union accepts no advertising or product samples and is not beholden in any way to any commercial interest. Its Ratings and reports are solely for the use of the readers of its publications. Neither the Ratings, nor the reports, nor any Consumers Union publication, including this book, may be used in advertising or for any commercial purpose. Consumers Union will take all steps open to it to prevent such uses of its material, its name, or the name of *Consumer Reports.*

This book is for my parents,
who showed me the way.

ACKNOWLEDGMENTS

I am grateful to my clients and the members of the Women's Institute for Financial Education who asked the questions about their own money that prompted this book.

I especially want to thank my former business partner, Carol McKeag, for her support over the years; W. Roberts Wood, for his gracious introduction into San Diego; and, most of all, Candace Bahr, for her continuing inspiration and ceaseless nudging.

Special thanks to Michael Larsen and Elizabeth Pomada, my agents, for helping me become an author, and to Kathleen Anderson and Sarah Uman for their editing skills.

CONTENTS

OUR MONEY
OUR SELVES

Introduction

Years ago, most women depended on men to manage their money. Today, whether you are single or married, widowed or divorced, you must be a skilled money manager to ensure your own economic survival. Financial responsibility is the path to female independence, and this guide to the facts of financial life for women is both a quick overview and a digest of the information you need to negotiate it best. Organized chronologically, in the order in which you are likely to encounter some of the financial crossroads most women's lives entail, it will show you how to proceed from the time you first embark on financial independence, through sharing your life with a partner, investing for the future, becoming divorced or widowed, and supporting yourself in retirement.

Beginning life on your own is exciting, exhilarating, and often daunting. This is an ideal time to begin a lifetime habit of budgeting and saving for your special needs. Saving, though not an end in itself, is an important means of acquiring luxuries and meeting financial goals. Shrewd money management, practiced early and consistently, will help you build a strong financial future.

Once you are working and on your own, it is time to begin building a credit history, which means planning your credit moves carefully. But no matter how carefully you save and how meticulously you establish credit, the crises of everyday life can intervene to present new financial challenges. Establish insurance plans that will cover medical expenses and protect your home, automobile, and other valuable personal belongings, and protect your earning power with disability insurance.

When you enter into a relationship with a partner, deciding to share your life with someone else, you may choose to live together before you marry. Some couples never marry at all. As you share your life, you will also be sharing your finances. You and your partner must decide how living costs will be split, how you will handle housing arrangements, and how property will be divided if you separate. If you decide to marry, you may need a prenuptial agreement that establishes your financial rights and responsibilities and the rights of both parties if the marriage ends. Every woman who marries needs to be aware of the financial realities of divorce or widowhood.

Deciding to bring a child into your life, either as an addition to a couple or if you are a single parent, requires not only physical and emotional adjustments, but a substantial financial adjustment as well. It means revising your financial planning to allow for the child's current needs, to pay for child-care costs, and to plan for your child's education. For example, you must protect your child's future by buying enough life insurance to fund continuing living expenses and future education costs.

As you mature, it is time to plan more specifically for the future. If you are young, retirement may seem far away. Of more immediate concern are long-term investments to support future financial needs, such as starting a business or funding your child's education and the costs of your first home. The qualities of a diversified investment portfolio are described and demystified, so that you will be able to develop the understanding and skills necessary to invest wisely and manage your investments with confidence.

In American society today, divorce has become a common reality of life at any age. At the turn of the century, the average marriage lasted for 18 years and ended in death. Now, although we are living longer, many marriages are not lasting, and over a quarter of all divorces take place among couples married for 15 years or longer. Divorce is never easy, but the more you know about your current financial position and your future financial needs and desires, the easier it will be to negotiate an equitable settlement. A realistic idea of what to expect in terms of future income and assets will help you pare expenses and adjust your life-style accordingly.

Children need financial support far beyond age 18, for example, but in most states child support payments decreed during divorce proceedings come to an end when the child reaches 18. Children are then presumed to be financially independent. Very few divorce settlements make any provision for a child's higher education, so it is generally up to the custodial parent, usually the mother, and unfortunately she is often the parent who is least able to make ends meet. As a consequence, for the first time in years, children are not receiving as much education as their parents. Taking steps now can protect your future and that of your children, even in the face of unanticipated divorce or the death of your partner.

While half of all marriages end in divorce, the rest end in death. More than 70 percent of the time, it is the woman who is left alone, a widow at the age of 56, the average age at which widowhood occurs. According to the Census Bureau, almost half of all married women over 65 will become widows and will outlive their husbands by an average of 18 years. If you begin as soon as possible to prepare for life on your own, you will be less likely to use money unwisely and more likely to be able to continue with the standard of living you prefer. To prepare for possible widowhood, you and your husband must have frank and open discussions about money. Having regular meetings to discuss your financial situation and the options available when one of you dies is one of the most loving gifts you can give each other.

Being on your own again often provides the opportunity to explore new career options. Increasing your job satisfaction with wise career moves will build both financial security and stronger self-esteem.

Whether or not you live with a partner, you are likely to be retired for as many years as those that passed before you took your first job. While Social Security benefits form a base for retirement, you will need to engage in careful planning so you can correct any shortfall between your expected retirement income and your actual needs, present and future. The details will include your considering a variety of options and establishing real figures so you can be aware of how you intend to accumulate resources and allocate them accordingly.

From the financial planning information that follows, you should be able to garner not only a good perspective about what to expect at each of the financial crossroads you may encounter, but also the understanding you need to negotiate them successfully, with knowledge and with confidence.

YOUR
MONEY STYLE

Economists say that money has value only in terms of its purchasing power in the exchange for goods and services. But for most of us, money has hidden meanings as well, and its meanings are bound up with our family backgrounds and our feelings of security, status, and self-worth. Consequently, our emotional attitudes toward money sometimes cause us to behave inconsistently and to use money in ways that are nonproductive and self-destructive: knowing we should save, for example, but going on a spending binge; knowing we should invest, but accumulating money in a low-interest-bearing savings account. When carried to extremes, this type of behavior can seriously endanger your financial life.

Because our attitudes toward money are shaped by so many predispositions, you may find yourself resisting as you read through portions of this book, saying, "Yes, but . . ." You may quickly recognize the inherent wisdom of the advice, but you may find that the specific suggestions offered somehow don't quite suit you. This response may be a function of your money style.

Once you understand the hidden factors that shape your attitude toward money, you may want to concentrate on altering some of your behavior. On the other hand, you may prefer not to adjust your own money style, but to understand it as a means of accepting that what is right for other people may, indeed, not be right for you. Either way, whether you modify your reactions or modify the advice to fit your individual money attitudes, you will have a clearer understanding of the role that money plays in your life. And the insight you gain from the characteristics noted, and from recognizing their potential sources, will be useful tools as you make financial decisions.

THREE COMMON MONEY STYLES

The profiles that follow are a bit simplistic, rendered in the extreme for quick recognition. Nevertheless, almost all readers will recognize aspects of themselves in one or more of them. Keep in mind that the categories are also useful in negotiating the more complex business of handling money with another person, whether mate or business partner. Here, a recognition of personal money styles can avert otherwise inevitable conflicts, confusion, and frustration.

THE BARGAIN HUNTER

◊ The Bargain Hunter is always in quest of her quarry, the big sale. Getting a bargain makes her feel great, but finding out there was a better bargain elsewhere makes her feel awful. She thinks about costs and discounts a great deal of the time, and sometimes buys things she doesn't really need simply because they are on sale. While this person takes pride in her bargain-hunting abilities, she may lack confidence in herself in other aspects of her life. She attempts to assert financial control of her life by focusing on details, and she is usually apprehensive about making mistakes.

In many ways, the Bargain Hunter has closed her eyes to money. Rather than looking at all aspects of her finances, she chooses to concentrate on price, and sometimes she sacrifices quality, suitability, and function in the process. She may have learned this behavior at home: Many Bargain Hunters grew up in families where their fathers handled the investments and their mothers were in charge of the spending.

Answer these questions to see if you are a Bargain Hunter.

1. Do you watch the sales more than you watch your personal finances?
2. When you shop, do you look for the best price you can get, even if the quality may not be the best?
3. Are you excited when you find a bargain, no matter how small the purchase?
4. Do you pay full price for things only if you absolutely have to?
5. When you discover you could have bought something elsewhere for less money, do you criticize yourself mercilessly?
6. When shopping, do you focus mostly on the money you've saved, rather than the money you've spent?
7. Do you make an investment because someone told you the product was underpriced, even if it doesn't fit your investment needs?
8. Do you react to hot investment tips without investigating them thoroughly, afraid you'll miss the opportunity to make a killing?
9. Do you spend a lot of time clipping and organizing coupons, compared to the money you save?
10. Do you sometimes buy things you don't need or want simply because they're on sale?
11. When people compliment you on your wardrobe, do you often tell them what bargains your purchases were?
12. Do you fret when you arrive at the grocery store and find you've left your coupons at home?
13. Do you delay buying things you want or need, hoping they'll go on sale next week?
14. Do you purchase clothing that doesn't quite suit you because it's on sale?
15. Do you sometimes stock up on a year's supply of things you don't really need?
16. Do you have a closet full of "bargains" you've never worn?

If you are a Bargain Hunter. Most of us who recognize ourselves in this profile often confuse our feelings about money with our feelings about our self-esteem. Bargain Hunters measure their accomplishments in terms of the bargains they have found, but all those accomplishments have to do only with money. If you are a Bargain Hunter, you can achieve a healthy balance by concentrating on seeking quality rather than focusing strictly on price. Direct your attention to qualities that have nothing to do with money or bargain hunting. If someone compliments you on your new clothing, for example, don't tell them what a buy it was, rather, say how much you liked the color when you first saw it. By concentrating on other attributes of your purchases and investments, you will begin to approach financial decisions in a more thorough way and be able to analyze your financial situation more fully. If you recognize yourself as a Bargain Hunter, take your overall role in earning and managing your money more seriously. Rather than seeking the next bargain, channel that energy into earning more money or investing more wisely, turning your preference for shrewd spending strategies into money in the bank.

If you are a Bargain Hunter, recognize that you enjoy the challenge of money, and expand your financial challenges to all aspects of your money situation, not just bargains. Tackle the challenges of achieving career satisfaction and integrating your financial goals. The point is to establish long-range objectives rather than concentrating on short-term spending goals.

THE SPLURGER

◇ The Splurger's credit cards are her best friends, but like some friends, they frequently talk her into spending money she can't really afford. Because she hates having to say, "I can't afford it"—after all, she works hard for her money, and she deserves to have money make her feel good, she believes—she often splurges when she's frustrated or feeling low.

If you recognize some aspects of yourself here, you may feel a great sense of frustration that your hard work has not garnered you more spectacular financial rewards. Rather than accepting what you have achieved or working harder to achieve more, you may spend what you have as a way of feeling more successful.

Splurgers are prone to fantasies of financial rescue, and those who have such fantasies fear achieving success on their own, afraid that they will give up a certain emotional dependency that has been keeping them from being self-supporting.

Answer these questions to see if you are a Splurger.

1. Do you think of credit cards as an absolute necessity, frequently spending to the limit and beyond?
2. When you go shopping, do you almost always buy more than you intend and often feel terrible as a result?
3. At the end of the month, are you always in debt?
4. When you feel anxious, bored, or angry, do you spend money to make yourself feel better?
5. If you inherited money, would you go on a spending spree?
6. Do you buy things you don't need or want because they are the "right" things to have or because they might impress others?
7. Do you feel inferior to others who have more money than you do?
8. Do you feel anxious or defensive when asked about your personal finances?
9. Do your spending habits lead to arguments with family members?
10. Do you carefully watch each penny, then suddenly find yourself squandering it away?
11. Does overspending make you feel more successful?
12. Do you spend money to compensate for the fact that you work so hard?
13. Do you use money as a way to punish or reward yourself?

If you are a Splurger. While money is tightly intertwined with the Splurger's definition of success, unfortunately, Splurgers never feel they have *enough* money, or seldom even have the perception of what money is.

For many Splurgers, money is also a measure of love and approval. The Splurger uses money to make herself feel good, but when splurging causes serious debt and undermines financial security, it is time to get a grip on it. If you share some of these characteristics, reward yourself for good performance with occasional splurges rather than spending binges. Or perhaps you can learn to enjoy making sound financial purchases: Splurge on some smart investments that will grow in value in the future, rather than on buying clothes you don't need. If spending is a social affair for you, join an investment club or attend financial seminars and networking groups, a good way of assuming financial responsibility.

If you are a Splurger, you probably also find yourself lavishing money and gifts on others. Instead, concentrate on building personal relationships on foundations other than money. Invest your time and your attention in your relationships with others, and invest your money in yourself. You will achieve considerably more satisfaction on both fronts.

THE MONEY HOARDER

◇ The Money Hoarder is deeply attached to her money. Her hobby is saving money, and she loves to see her bank account grow. She keeps her money "safe in the bank," never considering what that old pick-pocket, inflation, is stealing from her each day. In general, the Money Hoarder feels more pessimistic about her financial situation than the Bargain Hunter or the Splurger. She appears very successful, but she often worries that she may outlive her money and end up in poverty. This fantasy is a phenomenon so common that some financial planners have given it a name: The Bag-Lady Syndrome.

Women's changing financial roles often evoke pessimism and anxiety, even in people whose financial circumstances present absolutely no reason to be fearful. Those of us who have the characteristics of Money Hoarders do not feel in control of our financial destinies. Even those with the most secure, high-paying jobs and excellent health fear that their finances might evaporate, leaving them penniless and unable to earn the money back.

Here's how to tell if you are a Money Hoarder.

1. Do you think about money constantly?

2. Do you think that acquiring a lot of money would make you feel powerful?

3. Do you spend time fantasizing about winning the lottery, inheriting a large sum of money?

4. Instead of spending, do you feel most comfortable saving every penny?

5. Do you use money as a weapon to intimidate or attempt to control others?

6. Do you keep the bulk of your money in checking or passbook savings accounts?

7. Do you have difficulty making decisions about spending money regardless of the amount?

8. Does the thought of losing money paralyze you into indecision when it comes to investing?

9. Is money closely intertwined with your sense of achievement?

10. Do you feel that money is the only thing you can truly depend on?

11. Is your immediate impulse to say, "I can't afford it," whether you can or not?

12. When you need something, do you wait until it is absolutely necessary and then spend as little as possible?

13. Do you know almost to the penny how much money you have in your purse at all times?

14. Do you feel guilty about spending money for necessities such as a new pair of shoes for yourself?

15. Is the size of your bank balance so important to you that it sometimes governs your life?

16. Are you plagued with fears of a Depression?

17. Is it true that you can't imagine ever having enough in savings so that you wouldn't worry about the future?

18. Is your idea of a great vacation staying at home and counting the money you saved by not going anywhere?

If you are a Money Hoarder. With obvious exceptions, the Money Hoarder is onto a good thing. Financial security is essential for creating and building self-esteem. But too much hoarding can be destructive and can lead to internal turmoil and bitter conflicts with friends and family. If you find yourself deeply involved in the Money Hoarder style, you can take three positive steps. First, systematically examine your financial situation and assess your goals; then decide how much money you will need to reach your goals. Second, take more risk with your money, to gain greater rewards; make your money work as hard as you do. Don't take risks that will only increase your anxiety, but do take those that are sound and prudent. If it seems too good to be true, it probably is. Third, once you know what you need to reach your goals and you have your money working toward those goals, enjoy life! After setting your goals and both saving and investing for them, spend the remainder without guilt.

If you score strongly in the profile of a Money Hoarder, you may be making poor decisions regarding your money because you are overly concerned with safety, and you don't receive an adequate return on your money because of your fears. Pessimism about your future financial security may cause you to worry about money constantly and to become caught in an unhappy syndrome about controlling it. You can allay this tendency by consciously stopping your anxious thoughts every time they overwhelm you. If you must worry, then make an appointment with yourself to worry at a specified time each day. Then each time money anxiety creeps into your thoughts, you can tell yourself "Not now. I'll worry about that at seven o'clock tonight."

When your worry time arrives, make a list of all your concerns and decide what you can do to gain power over your financial situation. List the worst things that can happen to you and decide how you will deal with them. If you are worried about losing your job, create a plan now to reduce spending and increase your emergency savings. Financial experts recommend you save a minimum of three to six months' income. If you are worried that your mate might die and leave you penniless, review your insurance coverage and make appropriate adjustments. You will find that learning more about your money and working through the checklists and questionnaires in the Appendixes of this book will be very empowering. And once you have taken steps to gain power over your finances, you will realize that much of your worrying is without foundation.

If you share some of the characteristics of a Money Hoarder, make a list of all of the aspects of your financial life that are within your control. Instead of concentrating on the potential loss of your money, concentrate on your abilities to earn and manage money. Make a list of all the ways in which you deal well with money, such as in your work, in your personal spending, and in budgeting. Then make a list of the ways in which you feel inadequate in managing your money, and list ways you can overcome those inadequacies through gaining education and asserting financial control. Make that education your goal, and take the time to analyze your financial situation to overcome your money-hoarding tendencies and achieve greater peace of mind.

CONTROLLING YOUR MONEY STYLE

Being aware of your own basic money style will help you keep a balanced perspective. As the profiles make clear, their characteristics are damaging when taken to excess, and knowing one's tendencies can be a powerful corrective. Women with unhealthy attitudes toward money put off saving, budgeting, learning about finances, and thinking about the future, and they soon begin to find money a source of anxiety and worry. If your money style is so extreme that it has become an impediment, you can set positive financial goals to overcome the barriers that hold you back.

Following are eight steps you can take to increase your confidence and your ability to cope financially.

1. *Face the future.* Set short-term and long-term financial objectives, so you know, in a way that you can articulate, where you are going and how to get there. If you plan carefully, the future will take on more than the vague image it may have now.

2. *Keep current.* Keep current on your personal financial situation. Keep current on world events. Keep current on eco-

nomic trends. Your knowledge will enable you to change as times change.

3. *Seek financial freedom through education.* Increase your financial knowledge and perceptions. Then investigate opportunities and use your knowledge to solve financial problems.

4. *Save now, spend later.* Save your cash, and then invest it wisely. Project your future financial needs, and develop saving and investing habits that will meet those needs. Retirement planning is a must at any age.

5. *Take responsibility.* Don't depend on someone—mate, family, or friend—to rescue you. Chances are you will have to depend on your own financial resources for a major part of your life.

6. *Keep your perspective.* No matter what your problems are, other women have confronted them quite successfully. Get to know people who can help you, through seminars and networking groups, and enlist their aid on your behalf.

7. *Protect your earning power.* Your most valuable asset is your ability to support yourself, and by learning more about your career and your finances, you can develop and protect that important asset.

8. *Control your risk.* Manage your money to control your taxes and harness the positive power of inflation. Spend wisely, invest defensively, and diversify for more reward with less risk.

A HEALTHY APPROACH TOWARD MONEY

◇ Financial goal setting is the key to controlling your money style and keeping it healthy. If you don't have goals, you don't know how much you need to invest, or where to invest. Imagine your reaction if your best friend said, "I've got a surprise for you. I'm taking you on a two-week vacation, but I'm not going to tell you where. As a special treat, here's $5,000 for you to spend on clothes for the trip, but you can only take one suitcase." What would you buy with the $5,000? It would depend on where you were going, but if you don't know, how do you know what to buy? Your financial life can be just as frustrating if you don't have goals and know how you are going to accomplish them.

Once you set positive financial goals for yourself, you'll begin to believe that you deserve success and can accept the responsibilities of wealth, and you will never believe that having money is immoral or selfish. Your healthy approach toward money will cultivate sound financial management.

Here are the signs of a healthy approach toward money.

- You feel in control of money rather than being controlled by it.
- You use money in positive ways to enhance your life, not only as a means for providing necessities.
- You consider money a reward for accomplishment, not an end in itself.
- You can use money spontaneously on occasion without feeling guilty.
- You realize that money cannot solve all your problems.
- In your dealing with money, you adhere to your own general moral standards.
- You are aware of what money means to you and how you use it.

Your financial future is up to you. No matter what your past financial history has been, you can begin today to build a solid financial foundation.

ON YOUR OWN

MANAGING YOUR MONEY

Skillful money management includes controlling your expenses so that they don't exceed your income, increasing your income to keep pace with your expenses, and learning techniques for setting aside the money you need for emergency funds and long-term goals. By taking control of your money, you are substantially increasing your opportunities for achieving and sustaining financial success.

Now for the bad news: A plan for spending and saving money is a "budget," a word that makes many people cringe. But to say that someone is on a budget doesn't necessarily mean that they are deprived of most of the good things that money can buy. Just as "dieting" can be a rewarding plan for eating properly and enjoyably, so budgeting can help you realize your financial goals and make your life more comfortable and less stressful. Because the term "eating well" is more palatable than "dieting," let us here substitute the term "good money management" for the less appealing "budget."

ANALYZE YOUR INCOME AND EXPENSES

◇ To begin managing your money, it's best to gain a good historical perspective on your finances. You can do this by analyzing and understanding how you've used your money in the past, reviewing your financial records for the past 12 months, and cataloging your expenses by spending category, month by month. First take several pieces of paper and divide them into columns, heading each column with the appropriate expense category that applies to you. Here is a list of common expense categories:

HOUSING
  Rent or mortgage payment
  Homeowner's insurance
  Property taxes
  Utilities: gas; electricity
  Repairs
  Cleaning
  Telephone
  Furniture and appliances

FOOD
  Food and beverage
  Meals in restaurants

TRANSPORTATION
  Automobile payment
  Gasoline and oil
  Auto insurance
  Auto repairs
  Public transportation

HEALTH CARE
  Health insurance
  Doctors, dentists, other medical payments
  Drugs, toiletries

ENTERTAINMENT
  Movies, theater, concerts, etc.
  Hobby expenses
  Books and magazines
  Club memberships
  Vacations

DONATIONS AND GIFTS
   Donations
   Gifts

PERSONAL CARE
   Clothing
   Laundry and dry cleaning
   Personal care, haircuts, beauty products
   Child care and baby-sitting
   Children's allowances

LOAN PAYMENTS
   Credit card payments
   Other installment loan payments
   Interest expense

OTHER EXPENDITURES
   Life insurance
   Disability insurance
   Other taxes (not withheld)
   Education and tuition
   Attorneys, accountants, and other professional services
   Bank charges
   Savings and investments allocations
   Dues in professional organizations
   Miscellaneous

Now go through your checkbook for last month, and in each expense category list the checks that you have written and any withdrawals from automatic teller machines (ATMs) for the month. When you have listed all your checks and ATM withdrawals, add the expenses under each heading. Next, take a large sheet of paper, or tape two pages together. List your expense categories down the left side of the paper and the names of the months across the top, in 12 columns; leave 2 more columns for the annual totals and monthly averages. This is your summary sheet. Transfer the expense totals for the month to your summary sheet. Do this for each of the past 12 months. Then add the months together and put the totals in the next-to-last column. This column shows your expenses for the year. Divide the totals by 12, enter those numbers in the last column, and you will see what you spend on average each month for each category.

Be aware that as you compile your spending data, you may encounter some obstacles. Perhaps your check register is incomplete. If so, record your expenses from your canceled checks. But even if your checks are scrupulously recorded in your checkbook, your check register may not provide an accurate accounting. For example, if you use a bank card to draw cash from your bank account, write checks to the grocery store for more than the register amount, or if you receive cash back when you make bank deposits, your checkbook won't provide a record of where that cash is spent. In addition, your check register doesn't categorize by expense the payments you make on your credit cards. If you make only a partial payment on your bill each month, the amount of the check does not even reflect your total credit card charges for each month.

If your check register has these flaws, then when you analyze your expenses for the past year, add one expense category called "Cash" and another expense category called "Credit Card Payments." Your analysis won't provide you with quite as much useful data as it would if you knew the details within these categories, but for now, this method will suffice; in the future, be sure to keep track of these expenses so you build better financial records. Keep the detailed monthly billings that you receive from credit card companies so that you can record all your purchases each month by category, rather than only the lump-sum partial payment you make each month. And keep track of where your cash goes. Though this may seem like a great deal of work at first, keeping track of the cash you spend can be quite illuminating. Try it for one month. Keep a slip of paper in your wallet, and every time you pay for something, jot down what you bought and how much it cost before you leave the store or restaurant. After you do this for an entire month, review your list. You may be surprised at where your money goes. For example, your list of cash expenses may show that you are spending far more than you thought on fast food and snacks. If your cash expenses seem like a big hose siphoning out money that could be better used elsewhere, perhaps your list will give you the incentive to change your spending habits. At the very least, keeping track will make you aware of each expenditure as you make it.

In the future, when you record your expenses on your expense data sheet, you will be able to include a detailed breakdown of your cash expenses, and to keep better track of your credit card expenditures. Even if you pay only the minimum monthly amount due on each credit card, when you list your expenses for the month include every charge that appears on your credit card bill. And be sure to include the finance charge under the category for interest expense. If it adds up to a sizable chunk, that may give you the incentive to whittle down your charge card balances.

Once you have analyzed your spending history, analyze your income. If you are a salaried employee, this will be easy. If you are paid once a month, your monthly take-home pay is easy to establish. If you are paid twice a month, multiply your paycheck by 2 to figure monthly earnings. If you are paid every two weeks, multiply by 2.17. And if you are paid weekly, multiply your weekly paycheck by 4.33.

CREATING A SAVING AND SPENDING PLAN

◇ A great deal of money passes through your hands each year. If you earn and spend $2,000 a month, that amounts to more than a million dollars over your lifetime. Wouldn't you like to set some of that money aside for long-term goals, rather than letting it drift through your fingers? If you are having trouble saving money for long-term goals because no matter how much you make, your living expenses seem to escalate to meet your income, cut your income! Do it by socking away 10 percent of your current income into savings. Even if you haven't been able to save much in the past, you can begin now to build savings into your spending plan. Money that is deducted from your paycheck and deposited into a credit union account, 401(k) or other savings or stock purchase plan, or government savings bonds is money you are saving for the future. If your savings are earmarked for long-term goals such as retirement, consider investing in an individual retirement account (IRA) or an employer-sponsored retirement plan. That way, you'll reap tax benefits as well. If your goal is to save 10 percent of your income, and if 5 percent of your income already goes into one of the above plans, then you need to save only another 5 percent. One of the easiest ways to save is to initiate a forced savings plan, with a portion of your paycheck withheld and deposited by your employer directly without passing through your hands.

You are probably thinking, But I can't live on what I make now. Well, if you believe that you can't live on 100 percent of what you earn, then having only 90 percent of it to live on won't make much of a difference. While you certainly won't feel as though you are able to live on that amount either, at least you'll have something to show for all your hard work. If you'd like to feel that you are working for yourself, instead of working only to pay bills, then take a part of what you make and put it aside for yourself, and *then* adjust your expenses so that you can live on what's left over.

If, despite the lessons you learn about money management in this chapter, you really don't believe that you can afford to set anything aside, then tag future bonuses and raises for savings, as well as windfalls such as tax refunds, rebates, and cash gifts. Next time you receive a raise, deposit your pay increase into savings. Or ask your employer to deduct it from your paycheck and put it into savings for you, so that your net paycheck stays the same. Continue living on the same amount you earned in the past, and start on the road toward saving.

Let's assume that you want to save 10 percent of your income each month. Multiply your monthly income by 10 percent to compute the amount you will save each month. Now, subtract that from your income to find out what you will have left to spend. Compare your spendable income to the average monthly expenses you compiled. If your spendable income exceeds your expenses, you are living well within your means. But if your spendable income falls short, review your expenses to decide what economies you can effect in the future. Think critically about your expenses and you will find that some of the money you spend provides you with very little satisfaction. Expensive lunches, clothes bought primarily because they are on sale rather than being attractive, and unnecessary spur-of-the-moment expenditures are only a few examples of costs that are controllable. If you often spend on impulse and regret it later, resolve now to cut back on those types of expenses, and let your spending plan reflect that resolution.

When you are devising ways to trim expenses, be creative and examine all aspects of your life, from how you buy insurance to the

the expenditure on the piece of paper you keep in your wallet. This will soon become automatic, and by taking this extra step, you will begin to think critically about each expenditure rather than impulsively buying things you don't really need and may not even want.

Your spending plan is a unique reflection of you and your habits, needs, and desires. Where you spend your money is within your control, so consider your options carefully. If you call on your family to help, try not to impose too many stringent spending controls on family members at one time, or you may have mass mutiny on your hands. To keep the family peace, each member of your family should have some money that she or he can spend without being accountable to the budget. To allow for this, you may want to add an expense category in your spending plan called "individual allowances."

Count all the money you spend. If income from odd jobs or investments contributes to your living expenses, be sure to account for it in your spending plan. Don't let that money slip through the spending cracks; it has the same value as the money you receive from your regular employment. And if you receive a substantial amount of cash in the form of a bonus or an income tax refund, plan carefully what you are going to do with it, and stick to that plan. You may decide to spend part of it on something special you've wanted, such as a new appliance or a trip. Or you may want to earmark a portion for future goals or for long-term savings.

MONITOR YOUR PROGRESS

◇ Each year, you can assess your current net worth. (See Appendix 3.) By keeping track of your financial situation year after year, you will be able to see the progress you are making. First pinpoint where you are today by listing what you own and what you owe. For some assets, you may need additional information. For example, to obtain the current value of your home, ask a local realtor to provide you with some comparable sales data for your neighborhood. Check with your employer to see what your vested interest in your pension or profit-sharing plan is, and get the current balances for any IRAs that you own.

Now make a column called "Annual Changes," and record the amount that your assets increase in value each year, not counting additional savings and retirement plan contributions. For example, if your savings account earns approximately 5 percent interest, which you allow to accumulate in the account, and you have an average balance of $3,000, you earn about $150 a year. Write that amount in the "Annual Changes" column. If your house has been growing by 5 percent in value each year, multiply its present value by 5 percent and put that number in the "Annual Changes" column. Some assets, such as your car, decrease in value rather than increasing each year. List the amount by which your car's value will decrease each year in the "Annual Changes" column, with brackets around it to show it is a reduction. The amount of increase or decrease you anticipate for each of your debts also should be listed in the "Annual Changes" column. Once you have filled the column completely, add the positives and subtract the negatives; the result is the annual increase or decrease in your assets and debts. Add to that the amount that you are stashing in savings and retirement plans each year, and you now know how much your net worth is changing each year. If that number is positive, you are on the right road. If it is negative, you have some problems that need correcting.

WHERE TO PUT YOUR SAVINGS

Once you have begun saving money, you must decide where to put the cash you are accumulating for your emergency fund savings, investing, and the cash that you require for your current needs.

You have many choices in today's complex deregulated financial arena. For your savings, the safety of your money is paramount. Despite the continuing crisis in the savings-and-loan industry, which is now joined by increasing numbers of bank failures, your money is still safe if your bank or savings-and-loan is insured by the FDIC, which protects individual accounts up to $100,000 and joint accounts up to an additional $100,000. Credit unions are insured by the National Credit Union Share Insurance Fund (NCUSIF).

In addition to federally insured institutions, you might want to consider money market accounts offered through brokerage houses and mutual fund companies. A money market account is really a mutual fund of short-term money investments. These funds are not federally insured, but since they invest in only short-term instruments from institutions with high credit ratings, such as major corporations, large banks, U.S. Treasury obligations, and the like, they are generally quite safe.

Some money market funds and most brokerage houses offer asset management accounts, which place your money market fund, a checking account, your stocks and bonds, and a credit card under one umbrella. All your investment activities are detailed on one monthly statement, and the interest and dividends that are earned on your investments are automatically deposited into your money market fund. The minimum required investment for these asset management accounts range from $5,000 to $20,000, and annual fees are generally $75 to $100.

Your bank may offer a money market account as well, but it isn't a money market account in the true sense of the word. Generally, true money market funds pay much higher interest than bank money market accounts.

Other bank accounts available include passbook savings accounts, so called because you are issued a passbook into which your deposits, withdrawals, and balances are noted. These accounts usually pay a low rate of interest. You may also decide to employ an interest-bearing checking account, sometimes called a NOW account or a Super NOW account. Non-interest-bearing checking accounts generally charge a monthly or per-check fee, which can usually be eliminated by maintaining a specified minimum or average balance. The interest-bearing accounts may charge a fee, and usually don't pay interest if your balance falls below a certain amount. NOW and Super NOW accounts generally pay higher interest than the bank savings accounts, but sometimes limit the number of withdrawals you can make each month. Evaluate the characteristics of these different accounts and choose the one that is best for you. You may want to make a change if your financial condition changes.

When choosing a bank, consider the stability of the bank by reviewing the most recent annual statement of condition and quarterly call report, both of which your bank will gladly provide. First, check to see that the net income is positive, which means the bank is making money. Next, divide the shareholders' equity by the bank's total assets to see if the bank has enough equity to cover future losses. The equity should equal at least 5 percent of assets. Finally, compare the past-due loans to the bank's loan-loss reserve balances to determine if the bank has excess problem loans that will have to be covered by the bank's equity. A healthy bank will have reserves large enough to cover problem loans, but a bank whose excess problem loans exceed the bank's equity is headed for trouble.

When choosing a bank, also consider the convenience of the bank's branch locations. A bank with a branch near your office and your home, or in the grocery store where you shop, is particularly convenient. In fact, with automatic teller machines and ATM networks, almost any financial institution is convenient. But some banks charge fees for using their ATMs, and if you make a significant number of ATM transactions, the expense can become substantial.

One standard to use in deciding on which bank to use is whether the bank returns your canceled checks with your monthly bank statement. All banks are required to keep your checks on microfiche, but if the bank's routine does not include sending you your canceled checks each month, you will have to ask for copies of the checks when you need them. It is far more convenient to have the checks returned with the bank statement, and having them at hand will provide proof of payment and help you compile your income tax information.

Certain other banking services may also be important to you. They include the availability of safe-deposit boxes, MasterCard or VISA cards, notary services, and various types of loans.

Remember that when you put your money in the bank, you are making a loan to that bank, for however short a period of time. In exchange, you should receive a competitive rate of return on your money, and your bank should offer you both respect and service. In addition, the bank should give you a guarantee, through federal insurance and a healthy financial picture, that it will be able to repay your money when you demand it. If your bank is not giving you the service and respect you deserve, find another one.

Beware of interest rates that seem too good to be true. If a financial institution is paying a much higher rate of interest than its competitors, look beyond the interest to the risks. Is the institution federally insured? Is it on shaky financial ground and expecting a federal takeover, and thus needs to pay higher rates to attract depositors? If that is the case, stay away. If your deposits are insured, it is likely that you will get your money back if the institution is taken over, but you will be better off accepting a somewhat lower rate of interest and avoiding even the prospect of this situation. After all, if you can earn 1 percent more on your savings at a financially troubled institution, and your nest egg amounts to $10,000, that is only $100 per year additional interest, which amounts to 30 cents a day. Your peace of mind is certainly worth more than that.

BUYING INSURANCE

MEDICAL INSURANCE

◇ There is no greater catastrophe than serious illness, and without the protection of high-quality medical insurance, which includes both a basic hospitalization policy and a major medical policy, your finances can be wiped out in a short time. Unfortunately, both kinds of medical insurance are becoming more expensive each year, but it is still possible to cut costs while securing the kind of coverage you need.

If you are employed, you probably have medical and hospital coverage through your employer. If you are recently divorced or widowed, you will be eligible for temporary coverage through your former spouse's employer under a federal law called COBRA. The temporary coverage for a divorced or widowed person and her dependents is 36 months. The medical coverage is the same as when you were married except now you are responsible for the premiums.

At the end of 36 months, you will have to purchase an individual hospitalization policy and major medical plan. These policies are available through many private insurance companies and a variety of health maintenance organizations (HMOs).

For people not covered under an employer's plan, comparing the benefits of various major medical insurance policies is a complicated and often confusing business. First, look for a high upper limit, one that covers at least $1 million of medical expense before it stops paying. Next, compare the initial deductible—the amount of the bill you must pay before you start receiving benefits—and the co-insurance clauses, which require you to pay a percentage of costs above the initial deductible amount up to a certain limit. Then note the kinds of medical expenses that are either limited or excluded from coverage, such as dental costs, drugs, psychotherapy, cosmetic surgery, et cetera.

If you have capital reserves and are infrequently ill, consider a major medical policy with a high annual deductible. The deductible is the amount you must pay before the insurance company starts picking up the tab, and a high annual deductible will sharply cut premiums—the cost you pay for the policy—while the policy will still protect you against the ever-escalating costs of a serious, life-threatening illness.

Health insurance policies differ enormously from one another, each having its own limitations, qualifications, and exceptions. To analyze a policy, begin by listing your—or your family's—medical expenses for a typical year by types of expenses for each family member. Then, for each policy you are considering, estimate how many of these expenses you would be responsible for and how much the insurer would pay. This will give you an idea of the coverage you can expect in a typical year. Next, assume that you or someone in your family was in an accident and required hospitalization, extensive surgery, and on-going physical therapy. How many of these expenses would be covered by the insurance company, and how much would come out of your pocket? Add the cost of the insurance premiums to the medical expenses that you would have to bear in each scenario, and you will be able to compare the apples and oranges of each policy.

HMO coverage is often cheaper, but you must be able to be flexible about the restrictions HMOs impose on the use of non-HMO care. Evaluate HMO quality by asking acquaintances who are enrolled in the HMO about the quality of care and service. Investigate the reputation of the practitioners and the hospital your HMO uses. Be sure to consider convenience here, since a long hospitalization might require many trips by other family members to the care facility. Find out if the HMO requires a long wait for appointments, and what the arrangements are for emergency care. Once you have gathered all the information necessary to assess a medical plan, assume that you are in need of a variety of medical services, and then systematically evaluate how responsive each plan would be to your situation. You may wish to consult *Consumer Reports* Ratings of health insurance policies in the August 1990 issue.

AUTO INSURANCE

◊ If you drive, each state requires you to carry liability insurance for bodily injury, which protects you against claims if your car injures or kills someone. This bodily injury insurance is important, since if you are sued for damages by someone injured in an accident, it could wipe out your savings and throw you into bankruptcy court. In selecting auto insurance, it's therefore imperative to choose the highest limits available, unless you have no assets to protect, and if you live in a state where court awards are high, you might want to consider an umbrella policy to protect you in the event of claims above those limits.

You also need liability insurance for property damage, which pays claims for property damaged by your car. This coverage is usually linked to the bodily injury coverage, and the limits of the two types of coverage are expressed on your auto policy with three numbers, such as 100/300/50, which means that you are protected for $100,000 of claims for injury to an individual in an accident, $300,000 of claims for all individuals in that accident, and $50,000 of property damage.

Collision insurance covers the damage done to your own car in a collision. The higher the policy's deductible amount, which is the amount you pay for each accident, the lower the premium you pay for your collision coverage. The same is true of comprehensive insurance, which covers damage to your car from causes other than collision, such as theft.

Uninsured motorists coverage pays for accidents in which you are not at fault if the other party is uninsured. Most policies cover only bodily injuries, while others pay for damage to your car. Most auto policies also offer medical coverage, which provides for reimbursement of medical expenses resulting from an auto accident. Review your auto policy to make sure that the medical coverage you are paying for does not duplicate the coverage supplied by your health policy, and eliminate overlapping medical coverage to reduce premiums.

In addition to these basic coverages, most auto policies offer extra options such as towing insurance and rental-car reimbursement. Consider carefully whether the increased premium is worth the cost of such relatively infrequent events.

The general premium you pay for auto insurance is based on the individual insurer's assessment of risk factors regarding where you live, what your driving record is in terms of accidents, traffic violations, and previous insurance claims, and the kind and vintage of the car you drive. Shop around. Many policies offer discounts if you have taken a driver-training course, if your car is driven relatively infrequently, if you have no teenage drivers in your family, or if you fall into other risk-lowering categories.

HOMEOWNERS INSURANCE

◊ Whether you own a home or rent one, you need homeowners insurance to reimburse you in the case of damage sustained to your property and furnishings and in the event that someone is injured in your home. If you own your home, the insurance coverage you secure will be a homeowners policy, and if you rent your home you will be covered under a tenants policy. The basic coverage these policies provide protects you against loss from most common risks, such as fire, windstorms, theft, et cetera. For higher premiums, you can add additional protection for building collapse, falling objects, and damage from water, ice, or snow. A comprehensive policy will cover everything except damage caused by earthquakes, tidal waves, floods, war, and a few other such phenomena. If you live in a region that is vulnerable to one of these excluded risks, such as earthquakes, you can buy a supplemental policy that will protect you from these damages as well. Be sure to comparison shop and investigate a number of options; don't assume that every policy will supply the kind of or amount of coverage you need.

The premium you pay varies in accordance with the risk rating of your property, the amount of the deductible you choose, and the amount and type of coverage you require. The co-insurance clause requires you to insure your property for at least 80 percent of its replacement cost to maintain full insurance. If you insure your home for less than that, even unwittingly, you are accepting part of the liability if your property is damaged. You should buy enough insurance to cover the cost of rebuilding your house, excluding the land value and foundation cost. Remember that replacement costs increase with inflation, and keep reviewing your policy to keep your coverage up-to-date.

The best way to make sure your insurance is adequate is to buy a guaranteed-replacement-cost policy. The insurance company will adjust the amount of insurance each year, and guarantees that you will receive full payment on any claims, even if the cost of replacing your residence exceeds the face value of the policy.

DISABILITY INSURANCE

◇ Disability can wreck all your financial plans. At age 35, you are six times as likely to become disabled than to die during the coming year, and even in your early sixties you have a greater chance of becoming disabled than you do of dying, according to statistics compiled by the Health Insurance Association of America. Disability is often financially devastating, because when you are disabled your income will stop but your expenses will escalate. Consequently, you need disability coverage to replace such lost income in the event that you should become disabled.

Some employers provide disability insurance, but many do not, so chances are that you will need to purchase a private plan. If you are covered by the Social Security program, you already have limited disability coverage. The rules are narrow and strictly enforced. If the disability you suffer is expected to last for at least a year, and if you are unable to work at any job, you may begin collecting Social Security disability benefits after six months. But what are you going to live on for those six months? And what if you are unable to perform the job you were trained for and you don't wish to accept a different job? You need a disability policy that provides the kind of coverage that is omitted under the Social Security program.

Three factors affect the cost and quality of disability coverage:

how long the waiting period is until the policy begins paying benefits; how long the insurance company will continue to pay benefits; and how disability is defined. The longer the waiting period, the less expensive the policy. If your employer provides you with cumulative sick-pay benefits, you may be entitled to collect your regular paycheck for quite some time. Or perhaps you have enough savings to enable you to live for six months, so you can choose a six-month waiting period, which will make the coverage far less expensive. Choose a policy that will continue to pay benefits until you are age 65, when you can begin collecting your full Social Security. You may wish to consider coverage that pays benefits beyond age 65, but you probably will find such a policy to be prohibitively expensive.

Finally, look at the insurer's definition of a disability. The policy should cover you for any disability that renders you unable to work at your own job, and it should also insure you for the losses suffered if you decide to work at a less demanding job that pays less money.

UMBRELLA POLICIES

◊ If you have substantial property to protect and if liability awards are relatively high in your state, the liability insurance coverage included in your auto and homeowners policies may not be sufficient. If you are sued and a judgment is entered against you, the excess of that judgment over the limits of your policies must be satisfied out of your own assets, which could bankrupt you. Consider adding an inexpensive umbrella insurance policy to your coverage that begins where other liability policies end. An umbrella insurance policy will provide liability coverage of $1 million to $5 million, and in addition to insuring against liability for injury, it covers expenses sustained if you are charged with libel, slander, or invasion of privacy.

LIFE INSURANCE

◊ How much life insurance do you need? Life insurance should fill the gap between the nest egg you have accumulated and the money your dependents, your partner, or other survivors will need to continue their lives when you die and are no longer contributing to their support. If you are single with no dependents, your life insurance needs are negligible, and you may want to purchase only enough to cover whatever debts you have and your burial expenses. If you buy more life insurance than you need, you are wasting money, for there is no benefit to being worth more dead than alive.

When you assess your life insurance needs, consider the potential economic impact of your death on your survivors. For example, if you have a child who dies, you will certainly suffer greatly, but the nature of the suffering would not include financial distress, and it is therefore unlikely that you need to purchase an insurance policy on the life of your child. You do need insurance on *your* life, however, in case something happens to you before your child is self-sufficient or if your surviving mate were to be left in debt as the result of losing your income. (See Appendix D to determine how much life insurance you need.)

SHOPPING FOR INSURANCE

◇ If the worksheet indicates that you need more life insurance than you presently own, your next task is to find the right policy from the right life insurance company. The price of the policy is important, but the stability of the company and the policy's features are key. Look for a life insurance company that is financially sound. You don't want it to expire before you do, and since life insurance provides money to be received by your heirs upon your death, the company must be around to pay them when you die. Try to buy insurance from a well-respected company that is highly rated by insurance rating services such as A. M. Best. (However, even these services can be caught unaware of a company's insolvency, as the insurance company failures of the recent past have demonstrated.) Avoid dealing with smooth-talking agents whose desire for a sale is clearly greater than their interest in providing you with coverage that is appropriate to your particular needs.

Over the past 10 years, the life insurance industry has melded with the investment industry and has created a panoply of products that combine life insurance with investments. Those products go by a variety of different names, including universal life, variable life, and universal variable life.

TERM INSURANCE

◇ Term insurance is the easiest kind of life insurance to buy. You purchase it for a specified term, usually one year, and at the end of that term your insurance lapses unless you continue the policy by paying a premium for the next year. This seems so simple that you may wonder why anyone would buy another kind of insurance. The benefit of term insurance is its simplicity. The drawback is that a new physical exam may be required periodically, your premium will probably increase over time, and at some point the cost of the insurance may be beyond your reach. Of course, at that point in your life you may no longer need life insurance. This drawback can be partially controlled by buying level-premium term insurance that guarantees a fixed premium for a specified number of years. Make certain that any policy you buy is guaranteed renewable at least to age 65, unless you need coverage only for a short period of time.

Term insurance is your best bet if you need insurance for a limited period of time in a fixed amount. For example, if you have teen-aged children, you may want to buy insurance on your life to protect them until they are through college. After that, they will be on their own, and you may no longer need as much life insurance coverage. Or perhaps you are building a retirement nest egg and you need life insurance coverage only until your accumulated investments reach adequate size. If you and your mate have taken on a substantial mortgage or other loan, a life insurance payment could guarantee your part of the amount outstanding in the event of your death. In any case, if your insurance needs will dwindle over the years, term insurance will give you the coverage you need at the least expense.

WHOLE LIFE POLICIES

◇ Whole life insurance has been sold for many years. Its premiums remain the same for the whole life of the insured. Your policy builds up a guaranteed cash value, and if it is a participating policy, you may receive dividends as well. These dividends are not taxable to you since they are considered to be a return of excess premiums you have paid. While whole life has its virtues, in Consumers Union's views, most people can more affordably meet their insurance needs with term insurance.

UNIVERSAL LIFE POLICIES

◊ Universal life insurance generally pays a more competitive interest rate on the investment portion of your life insurance policy than whole life policies do. It also offers adjustable features that allow policyholders to change the face amount or the premium level to suit their changing needs over the years. A universal life policy might suit you if the portion of your money that buys the actual insurance and the expenses within the policy compare favorably with the cost you would pay for term insurance, if you have extra income with which to fund the policy, and if you could earn a greater after-tax rate of return within the universal life contract than your money is earning for you now. Other types of investments, however, may provide even better returns on your money.

Universal life policies have several drawbacks:

- The interest rates paid are adjustable ones that fluctuate along with prevailing interest rates; like banks, insurers may offer a high interest rate to attract buyers, and then lower it substantially.
- The mortality rates and expense charges may rise within the contract, increasing the cost of the insurance portion of the policy and decreasing the amount available for investment.
- Policyholders must decide each year how much to invest in the policy.
- Universal life policies are governed by a maximum funding level imposed by the Internal Revenue Service, which means that policyholders cannot increase the investment portion of their accounts without increasing their life insurance coverage.

VARIABLE LIFE INSURANCE

◊ With variable life insurance, both the death benefits paid and the cash values vary to reflect the investment results of the insurance company. Variable life insurance gives the policyholder the opportunity (and accompanying risks) of investing in a variety of investment products that include money market accounts, stock funds, bond funds, guaranteed interest accounts, and real estate funds. With a variable life policy, you can spread your annual investment among these accounts and move your money around from year to year without incurring income taxes.

Variable life has drawbacks as well:

- Once you have purchased the policy you cannot change the amount you pay.
- The premium is much higher than that required by a term insurance policy.
- Though it is technically a life insurance product, variable life falls into the category of a tax-advantaged investment, which means Congress can modify or eliminate the advantage of tax-free investment buildup at any time.

Another variation is universal variable life, which is much like variable life, except that both its face amount and premium payments are flexible.

APPLYING FOR CREDIT

When you begin applying for credit, the easiest place to start is to apply for a department store credit card. Many stores allow you to open an account when you are making a purchase. Once you have a department store credit card in your own name, you should be able to qualify for a gasoline credit card. With a department store charge account and a gas card, a bank card such as MasterCard or Visa is within reach. Once you have all three, you can apply for a travel-and-entertainment card such as American Express or Diner's Club. The fact that you qualify for a travel-and-entertainment card has special clout when a potential creditor is assessing your bill-paying performance, since these cards require their cardholders to pay their balance in full each month.

Fill out your credit card applications completely and accurately. In the space requesting salary information, be sure to list your gross salary *before* any withholdings. When listing your assets, supply their current value, not their original cost.

How Credit Is Granted

◇ When you apply for a credit card or charge account, the lender scores your credit application and bases its decision on the results. The scoring varies from lender to lender, but here are some of the categories that lenders consider.

1. *Income.* Generally, the higher your income, the more points you score in the rating system. It is important to include all your income, from whatever source, on your application.
2. *Existing debt.* You are not likely to be granted credit if your monthly debt payments exceed 35 percent of your gross income.
3. *Other credit cards and loans.* You will receive many points on the scoring system if you have had a loan with the same lender in the past and have repaid on schedule. You will also score points for some travel-and-entertainment cards, bank cards, and department store charge cards, and a favorable credit history on other loans will help as well. But be careful about amassing too many credit cards. If you have too much available credit it may count against you.
4. *Length of time at residence.* Generally, you will score more points the longer you have been at your current address, but with the increasing mobility in our society, you probably will not be downgraded for a recent move.

5. *Occupation.* You will score higher for a professional occupation than you will for a clerical one, and a technical job will score higher than an unskilled job. If you have a choice, describe yourself as an executive assistant rather than a secretary.
6. *Owning your home.* You will score higher if you are a homeowner than if you are a renter, but as home ownership has become less affordable, this category is becoming less important.
7. *Bank accounts.* Since most people now maintain checking and savings accounts, having accounts in this category does not add as many points to your score as it did in the past.

If you are turned down for a credit card or a loan, you have the right to ask for a copy of your credit report within 30 days after your application is rejected. To do so, write to the credit agency named on the letter denying you credit, and ask them to send you a copy of the report. Enclose the letter from the lender that states you were denied credit based on a report issued by the credit agency.

Once you receive your credit report, review it for errors. If you find erroneous information in your file, ask the credit bureau to investigate the questionable item and make changes. The credit agency is required by law to investigate any errors that you discover. If they find that you are correct, they must revise the information in their files and notify anyone who received your credit report within the previous six months that erroneous material was contained in that report. If the credit agency cannot verify the error and refuses to change the information, you may write a 100-word explanation to be put into your file that must be included any time the credit bureau provides a report on your file.

Beware of credit clinics that offer to repair your credit record. In exchange for charging you a high fee, they will simply send requests on your behalf to the credit agencies, asking them to investigate questionable items. You have no assurance that the credit agency will find that an error has been made and delete the information from your file, and you certainly do not need to retain a credit repair clinic to dispute credit bureau information.

CREDIT DISCRIMINATION

◇ The Equal Credit Opportunity Act of 1977 forbids a creditor from discriminating against you on the basis of race, color, national origin, sex, marital status, or age. If you believe a creditor has discriminated against you, send a letter outlining the facts and the reason you believe you should not have been rejected for credit to the head of the department that denied you credit, and send copies to the president of the company, the attorney for the company, the Federal Trade Commission, and the Department of Justice, noting at the bottom of the letter that copies are being sent to these organizations.

The Equal Credit Opportunity Act requires that potential creditors respond to your completed credit application within 30 days. If you have applied for credit but have received no response, send a copy of your credit application to the head of the department with a reminder that a response is required by law within 30 days. If your application is subsequently rejected, promptly ask for the specific reasons on which the denial was based. The law requires that specific reasons be furnished to you, such as "insufficient income," "excessive obligations," "length of employment," et cetera. An explanation such as "You don't meet our standards" is not acceptable.

If your credit or charge account is revoked, or simply not renewed when it expires, you are entitled to know why. In addition, the reason given must be specific and nondiscriminatory. You cannot be denied credit simply because of a change in your marital status. (See chapter 7 for more about establishing credit.)

INCOME TAXES

ORGANIZING YOUR TAX FILES

◇ Whether you prepare your own tax return or employ a professional tax preparer, you will need to compile an accurate listing of your income and deductions. Although compiling tax information can be an unpleasant and time-consuming task, it is not really difficult. If you are employed, your employer will send you a Form W-2 by January 31 that shows your wages and withholdings from the previous year. If you are paid on commission with no withholdings, your income will be reported to you on a Form 1099. You will also receive a 1099 form for other payments, such as interest and dividends. If you receive Social Security benefits, the federal government will send you an annual report of your earnings. For pensions and other retirement benefits, you will receive a Form W-2P, showing income and withholdings. If you sold real estate or stock or other investments during the year, you will receive 1099 forms from the escrow agent or stockbroker. Remember that you must declare all taxable income that you have received during the year from whatever source, *even if you did not receive a reporting form from the payer.* If you received a check in December but did not deposit it until after January 1, it is still taxable income to you for the year in which you received it, not the year you deposited it into your bank account.

Review the deductions you claimed on last year's tax return and study the tax forms for the current year. Then sort through your monthly bank statements and remove from each statement the canceled checks representing tax-deductible items. Be sure to review your January bank statement to remove checks written in the prior year that had not cleared by the beginning of the new year, since they are deductible for the year written. Sort the deductible checks into groups, such as donations, taxes, medical and dental, interest, and miscellaneous deductions. Locate the receipts for bills that you paid with cash, and place them together with the canceled checks. Total the checks and receipts for each category, and transfer these totals to a list of your tax-deductible items.

After summarizing your tax data, insert the checks and receipts into envelopes and file by category. Place all the envelopes in a large manila envelope labeled "199_ Tax Information." The checks and receipts will then be readily available in proper order in the event of a future tax audit.

Most tax preparers base their fees on the amount of time that is required to prepare your tax return. By summarizing your tax information, you will greatly reduce the time required to prepare your tax return, and the savings in preparation fees will be well worth the additional time that it took to prepare your tax summary.

HOW LONG SHOULD YOU KEEP TAX INFORMATION?

◇ You are required to keep the records that substantiate your income and deductions available at all times for inspection by the Internal Revenue Service. This doesn't mean that you have to keep your records instantly available in case someone from the IRS knocks on your door, but upon reasonable notice from the IRS, you must be able to produce the records for an audit.

You must keep your records for as long as their contents may be material in the administration of any Internal Revenue law. Except in the case of fraud, the statute of limitations is three years from the due date of the return or the date of filing, whichever is later. The Internal Revenue Service may not audit any of your records beyond that date, but you should retain the following list of records for a longer period of time, even though the statute of limitations has expired.

1. *Prior tax returns.* Copies of your prior tax returns should be retained permanently. Not only are they helpful in preparing future tax returns and in making computations if you later file a claim for a refund, but they may also be of value to the administrator of your estate after your death.

2. *Payment of taxes.* To prove you paid your taxes when they were due, retain your canceled checks for tax payments with the tax returns to which they correspond. The IRS has been successful in collecting additional taxes from taxpayers who maintained that they had paid their taxes, but who were unable to prove it. Sometimes the IRS misplaces payments, and you should always be able to offer proof that you paid your taxes when due.

3. *Basis of property.* Records relating to the cost or other basis of property and improvements should be retained for as long as you own the original or replacement property. If you sold

your residence but deferred the tax on the gain by reinvesting in a new house, you will need to retain the records for both the new house and the old house. If you have sold several houses over the years, you may have several records to retain. Streamline it only to the extent that you keep one copy of all pertinent documents, including invoices, canceled checks, and records of cash disbursements.

In any of these categories, there is no reason not to retain your records permanently, so long as you have the room.

HOW TO DEAL WITH THE IRS

◇ Only 1 percent of all tax returns are audited each year, and even if you are audited, you should encounter few problems if you have reported all of your income and have kept careful records of your deductions.

The IRS may send you a notice requesting additional information, called a Document Matching Notice, if the information reported by payers on W-2s and 1099s does not match what you reported on your tax return. If you find that the payer has made an error, supply the payer with the proper information, and then outline your request in a letter to them, asking that they issue a corrected form to you. Then send this form to the Internal Revenue Service, along with a letter of explanation. If the payer is not able to correct the information, send the IRS a letter of explanation with whatever documentation you can present. If you do not do this promptly, the IRS computer will automatically churn out a second, more threatening notice. If you receive the second notice, circumvent the computer by calling the IRS and talking with a staff person.

Your return may be selected for either a correspondence audit or an office audit. For a correspondence audit, the IRS will ask you to mail them documentation of one or two items on your tax return. For an office audit, the IRS will send you a letter listing a number of items they want to audit, and they will give you a telephone number to call to schedule the audit. Do not ignore this notice. If you do not schedule an appointment, the IRS will disallow all items they have selected for audit and you will receive a very large bill for taxes, interest, and penalties. When it comes to income taxes, you are considered guilty until proven innocent.

If you are selected for an office audit, you may represent yourself, ask someone to accompany you, or ask a tax professional to represent you. Most taxpayers choose to go it alone, although it is certainly less stressful to send a representative, if you can afford it. For routine substantiation matters, you will save professional fees by representing yourself, but for anything more complex that requires interpretation of the law, you will fare better with a tax professional representing you.

Appear for your audit with your records in neat and orderly form, and avoid becoming riled. Most auditors respond favorably to politeness and a businesslike demeanor. Do not attack the U.S. tax laws as being unfair, and do not accuse the government of discriminating against you or wasting your money. The auditor is charged with enforcing the laws as they stand; don't take a chance that he or she will interpret your remarks about injustice or fiscal waste as a comment on the motives of the people who work for the IRS.

To best limit the potential avenues that the auditor might pursue, do not volunteer information. Try to be responsive to the auditor's questions, and to present your material in a methodical way.

If the auditor determines that you owe additional taxes, you will have to pay the taxes plus interest. Penalties are assessed only on the basis of negligence or fraud, and if you can persuade the auditor that you made an honest mistake and were neither negligent nor had intentions of defrauding the government, the IRS may not assess penalties against you.

Be sure not to ignore communications from the IRS and don't try to bluff your way out of paying additional taxes. If your contact with the IRS does not go smoothly, or if you disagree with the auditor's findings, you may want to bring in a tax professional who is experienced in representing clients at audits. A tax professional can provide you with the guidance to minimize the taxes, interest, and penalties you must pay. If you use a tax preparer who is not experienced in representing clients at audits, look elsewhere.

HOW TO CHOOSE A TAX PROFESSIONAL

◊ If you do not want to prepare your own tax return, you will need professional help. If you are salaried and have only a few itemized deductions, with little that is more complex, a reputable local preparer may be sufficient for your needs. If your situation is more complex, look for a CPA or an Enrolled Agent to prepare your tax return. A CPA has passed a three-day examination and is certified to practice public accounting in your state, and an Enrolled Agent has passed an examination administered by the Internal Revenue Service. Both CPAs and Enrolled Agents are qualified to represent you at an IRS audit. Ask for recommendations from friends whose tax situations are similar to yours. Before January, contact those professionals who were recommended and set up an appointment to interview them. Select a preparer who inquires about the details of your financial life, thereby securing as much information as possible to prepare your tax return. The preparer should be willing to explain tax matters to you clearly in language you understand. Beware of preparers who tell you the tax laws are too complex for you to understand, or who encourage you to sign your tax return without reviewing it. A tax preparer should suggest ways to reduce your taxes in future years and should be available to help you implement that advice.

LOANS AND BORROWING

When you shop for loans, compare the interest rates charged by each of the lending institutions available to you. The rates may be expressed as simple interest rates, variable or add-on rates, or discount rates, but for several decades the Truth in Lending Act has required all rates to also be expressed in terms of the annual percentage rate (APR), so you can compare them more easily. When you borrow money some lenders charge points, which are additional amounts, figured at 1 percent of the loan amount per point, that you pay "up front." Some loans also impose a prepayment penalty, which means that an additional amount will be added to the principal if you want to repay the loan early. This prepayment penalty is not included in the APR, and if you know that you will be paying off the loan early, you will have to add this penalty to your cost of borrowing money when you are comparing rates. Other hidden borrowing costs are loan application fees, appraisal fees, and, in the case of mortgages, inspection fees, the fees charged for title searches, and bank attorney fees.

AUTO LOANS

◇ If you are financing a new car, shop carefully for an auto loan. You must find the best rate and then decide on the term of the loan. Years ago, all cars were financed over a period 24 to 36 months. Now it is not uncommon to see auto loans of 72 or even 84 months. This does not mean that cars are lasting longer; the terms over which vehicles can be financed have been increased to reduce the amount of monthly payments and to attract borrowers. To save on interest charges over the life of your loan, choose the shortest term you can afford. And to save even more in the future, after you have finished making the payments to the financial institution, continue making the payments into your own bank account. In another few years, you will have accumulated enough savings to be able to pay cash for your next car, thereby avoiding paying costly, nondeductible interest in the future.

HOME EQUITY LOANS

◇ To consolidate debt and for other purposes, a home equity credit line can sometimes be useful, but it must be used with extreme caution or you could lose your home. If you own your home, you can establish a credit line for up to 80 percent of its appraised equity, and then borrow from your credit line by writing checks. You will be charged interest at an adjustable rate on the money that you borrow, and many loans allow you to pay only interest for the first 10 years. Read the fine print and know what you're signing. On home equity loans of $100,000 or less you are allowed to deduct the interest on your tax return. While this is a benefit—the interest you pay on auto loans and credit cards is not deductible—you must be certain to repay a home equity loan over a reasonable period of time. Although not a good practice, some people borrow on their home equity line for autos and vacations. The next year they take another vacation and borrow again, and the year after that they trade the old auto for a new one and borrow again to finance the new car. After a number of years they have borrowed the money for a dozen vacations and a half-dozen cars, and they face a large balance due on their home equity line, and the possibility of foreclosure if it cannot be met. If you believe you might not be able to repay such a loan before you get into financial difficulty, you will be far better off financing your new car with an auto loan and saving money regularly to pay for your vacation.

IF YOU HAVE FINANCIAL DIFFICULTY

◇ Some people make a habit of paying their bills in full upon receipt, thus avoiding interest charges. Others are not so disciplined and incur heavy interest charges on their overextended credit cards. When credit card spending gets out of control, these borrowers find themselves in serious financial difficulty, unable to pay more than the minimum monthly amount due. While most of us worry about debt from time to time, for others debt is a constant problem. If your current debt is giving you headaches, control it now before it gets out of hand.

Here are some warning signs that you need help in controlling your credit habits:

- You think of credit card balances in terms of the monthly payment and the credit limit available, rather than the total amount you owe.
- You don't keep track of your credit card expenses.
- You buy groceries and other such necessities at stores where you can charge your purchases on a credit card rather than using cash.
- You borrow from one credit card to pay off another.
- You are routinely one to three months behind on payments.

To control debt, begin at the beginning. While debt sometimes accumulates suddenly—after an illness, a job loss, a business setback, or an expensive lawsuit, for example—most people who go into debt do so slowly and hope the problem will take care of itself. In cases of serious debt, many people borrow to make payments on the ever-escalating bills. Eventually the problem becomes self-perpetuating, and there seems to be no way out.

If you are getting deeper into debt each month, reverse the trend now. Begin by making a list of everything you owe, the interest rates being charged, when payments are due, and the minimum payment amounts due. Now take the budget information that you created earlier in this chapter and add to it the minimum payments due on your debt. Compare your total expenses, including credit card payments, to your income. If your expenses are greater than your income, resolve now to put a stop to your spending, and begin paying off as much as you can on your debts. Each month pay at least the minimum amount, and then a few dollars more. Try rounding your payment up to the next $25 or $50. If you use your credit cards for purchases during the month, add the monthly charges to your payment. Do this faithfully month after month and your debt will shrink and gradually disappear.

To make room in your budget for these credit card payments, you must cut expenses. Reduce your living expenses by chopping away entertainment, restaurant meals, and anything else you can possibly live without. This temporary austerity is necessary in order to break the debt cycle before it can lead to bankruptcy. Consider even larger cuts, such as disposing of vehicles or selling your home and moving to less expensive quarters.

After you have pared expenses to a minimum, if you still cannot make ends meet, you must find ways you can increase your income. Look for a better-paying job or take a second job, perhaps one you can do at home, to supplement your income. Rent out a room in your house. Baby-sit for neighbors. If you have older children who are still living at home, ask them to find part-time employment so that they can contribute toward household expenses.

If you have increased your income and you still can't make ends meet, find ways to reduce your monthly debt payments. You may be able to borrow from relatives or friends at a low monthly rate of interest.

Explaining your situation to your creditors is often helpful. Some creditors are willing to adjust your payments if they believe you are sincere in wanting to repay your debts and that you have established a schedule to do so and intend to honor it. Contact the local office of the Consumer Credit Counseling Services, a debt-counseling service that has been formed by lending institutions to help people work out their debts. Once your creditors know you are dealing with the Consumer Credit Counseling Services, they probably will halt any collection procedures that may have been initiated and will work with you and your counselor to formulate a repayment plan you can live with. If you decide to use the Consumer Credit Counseling Services, a notation will be made on your credit report that you have done so. Even though you work your way out of debt, that notation will stay in your file and will indicate to potential future lenders that you had a problem with excess debt in the past.

PERSONAL BANKRUPTCY

◊ If your financial situation is drastic, you may want to consider personal bankruptcy. In bankruptcy, you file a petition with the bankruptcy court that suspends all payments while you devise a plan for repayment. You can file for personal bankruptcy under either Chapter 7 or Chapter 13 of the federal bankruptcy law. Under Chapter 13, referred to as the wage-earner plan, you will work out a plan for the repayment of debts over a number of years. Any debts remaining after the scheduled payments have been made will be discharged. Under Chapter 7 bankruptcy, otherwise known as a "straight bankruptcy," your assets will be liquidated and used to pay debts. Chapter 7 bankruptcy will eliminate most debts with the exception of the following, which are considered nondischargeable:

- state and federal taxes
- child support
- alimony
- student loans that became due in the past five years

- traffic tickets and criminal violations
- debt for credit purchases of $500 or more for luxury goods or services purchased within 40 days of your bankruptcy filing
- credit purchases or loans of more than $1,000 made within 20 days of bankruptcy filing
- loans obtained fraudulently

With these and a few other exceptions, after bankruptcy, any debts remaining will be extinguished.

You can choose to exempt some property under either federal or state law before your assets are liquidated. The laws differ from state to state, but most states allow you to keep some equity in your house and car, furniture and household goods worth less than $200 per item, a small amount of jewelry and tools of your trade, life insurance, and such retirement benefits as IRAs.

Though you may file for bankruptcy yourself, you will probably be better off hiring an attorney who specializes in debtor bankruptcy to help you through the process. By using a knowledgeable attorney, you will ensure that you exempt as many of your assets as possible and successfully fight any legal challenges to the bankruptcy. If you choose to file for bankruptcy on your own, books on do-it-yourself bankruptcy are available in public and business libraries, and the necessary forms are available from the bankruptcy court clerk. As you fill out the forms, make sure that you list all of your debts. If you fail to do so and omit a creditor, that debt will not be discharged in bankruptcy.

The bankruptcy process will generally take about six months, from the filing of the petition to the discharge hearing.

If your credit problems are not devastating, do not file for bankruptcy. Bankruptcy is your best option only if:

- You are facing foreclosure on your home that you can't forestall.
- Your dischargeable debts are at least one-third of your annual income.
- You don't have additional debts coming up in the future.
- You will be able to make ends meet after bankruptcy.

Do *not* file for bankruptcy if:

- You have filed for bankruptcy within the past six years.
- You have a large number of nondischargeable debts of the kind noted earlier.
- You expect additional large debts in the future, such as hospital or medical bills.
- Your debts are small in comparison to your income.

You can file for bankruptcy only once every 6 years, and the information will be reported in your credit file for 10 years. Although many creditors look unfavorably on past bankruptcies, this is not always the case. If your credit history includes a bankruptcy due to a crisis beyond your control, such as a major illness, and if you have had no problems in paying your bills since that time, then be sure to attach a note to your credit application explaining the situation when you apply for credit. If your bankruptcy was under Chapter 13 and you paid back a great many of your debts, that history may be looked upon more favorably than a Chapter 7 straight bankruptcy. If your bankruptcy was under Chapter 7 and all your debt was discharged, you may be considered to be a good credit risk, since you owe no money and you are unable to declare bankruptcy for another 6 years. (See chapter 3 about declaring bankruptcy if you are married.)

Sometimes bankruptcy as a legal state can offer you the kind of protection you need in order to begin establishing a sound financial foundation. If you are unable to afford a private attorney who is experienced in counseling about bankruptcy matters, then see what kind of nonprofit legal assistance is available in your community. In either case, try to locate the kind of attorney who will be able to spend time with you and consider your case with care, not a harried practitioner who is unable or unwilling to give you the kind of careful representation you need.

SHARING YOUR LIFE

LIVING TOGETHER AND MARRIAGE

Couples living together without being legally married is an increasingly frequent situation for a number of reasons today; remarriages also are on the rise. Understanding the legal and financial ramifications of your living arrangements is, therefore, particularly important. Couples should determine in advance cost-sharing arrangements while they are living together, prenuptial agreements concerning cost-sharing while married, and their asset and debt division when the marriage ends, as well as clarifying all matters about inheritance.

For example, if you are living with someone in a committed but unwed state and he dies without a will, everything he owns will pass to his next of kin, and you will have no legal claim on it. If the two of you were married at the time of his death, the bulk of his property would probably have passed to you. If you do not want to bother with drawing up contracts and agreements that protect you, you are probably financially better off getting married, if otherwise feasible, and accepting the protection of the marriage contract your state writes for you. That way, you will inherit most of your partner's assets when he dies at no estate tax cost, you may be covered under his health insurance policy, and you can take advantage of state laws regarding property division and spousal support if your marriage ends in divorce. In addition, in the event of his serious illness you will be consulted for medical decisions and granted hospital visiting privileges, you will be entitled to Social Security survivor benefits if he dies, you will qualify for his pension benefits, and any children born of your relationship will automatically belong to both of you without taking extra steps to acknowledge the paternity of the child. Though some of these benefits may be available to you by making specific provisions in a legal contract, that contract is subject to challenge by other potential claimants.

Unfortunately, documenting your arrangements in a contract is not very romantic. We may remember our first date, our first kiss, and the first night we spent together, but no songs have been written in tribute to the first contract we signed. The beginning of a relationship seems to be a particularly inappropriate time to think about such an agreement, but once the relationship takes on stability, it's time for you to come to an understanding about these matters with your partner and to document them legally.

LIVING-TOGETHER AGREEMENTS

◊ A written living-together agreement will make it very clear what was intended if your relationship disintegrates later. Though the document can be simple, you will probably want to enlist the services of an attorney to ensure that the document correctly expresses your intentions, and that you haven't omitted any critical sections. The agreement does not need to be filed into the public records, but each party to the agreement should keep an original signed copy in his or her files or safe deposit box, for use if a dispute arises later.

Before you can put your agreement in writing, you have to reach that agreement. You must decide who owns what, how property will be divided if you separate, whose debts are whose, and how household expenses will be split while you are living together. Some living-together agreements also call for marriage within a specified time.

If you decide to live together without a formal agreement, or if you find yourself doing so without having so decided, the safest thing you can do is to own nothing in common with your partner. Don't

share bank accounts or credit cards unless you have a clear understanding, preferably in writing, about how the balances will be
divided. And remember that credit and financial institutions are not
bound by your private agreements. If you have both signed on a credit
card, you are both 100 percent responsible for all charges made. If you
both share a single bank account and the IRS seizes your partner's
funds for back taxes, your money will disappear along with his.

Many couples decide to share living expenses 50–50, but if there
is a disparity in your relative incomes, a proportionate sharing may be
fairer. Also consider the costs for children who are a part of the
arrangement. If they are your partner's children from an earlier marriage, he will probably pay for their clothing, entertainment, and
allowances from his separate funds. But what about the food they eat
at your table? How is the grocery bill shared? These are mundane, yet
sticky, issues, and they frequently give rise to frustrations and anxi-
eties regarding the role of the children in the relationship. It is far better to raise these issues and to discuss them in advance than to let them
fester, and creating a living-together agreement is the best way to cod-
ify your discussions.

Housing is a particularly important issue for people who are living together. Whether you rent or buy, you will have to put your
name on a legal contract, either a deed or a lease. Will you sign the
document together? If so, what are the rights of either party if you
break up and one of you moves out? And what are the legal ramifications, especially on a lease that both of you have signed together?
These are questions you must decide in advance.

With the current structure of the tax tables, it is cheaper to live
together than to marry. For example, if you each earn $50,000 a year
and claim the standard deduction, your tax would be $9,560 each, a
combined tax of $19,120. If you were married, your combined tax
would be $20,465. As you can see, it costs $1,345 in income tax for
the privilege of being married for the year. The only time that it is
more beneficial for tax purposes to be married than single is if only one
of you works and you file a joint tax return, since the joint return rates
are lower and an exemption would be claimed on it for the nonwork-
ing spouse, as well as for the working spouse. Of course, if two people
live together and one supports the other, the working partner may
claim a dependency exemption for the other, if he or she provides

more than half the partner's support and the partner earns less than $2,300 a year. Still, a dependency exemption will not be available if the state in which the couple resides makes cohabitation illegal, and these laws still exist in many states today, including Arizona, Idaho, Mississippi, North Carolina, and Virginia.

PRENUPTIAL AGREEMENTS

◇ If you are happy with the financial marriage contract that your state has written for you, and you are willing to keep track of your separate assets and liabilities (if you want to keep them separate), you may not need a prenuptial (premarital) agreement.

But first, you must know what the laws of your state specify about your financial rights in marriage. If you are in a state with community property laws, then the law requires an equal division of community property accumulated during the marriage in the event of divorce. (The community property states are Arizona, California, Idaho, Louisiana, Nevada, New Mexico, Texas, Washington, and Wisconsin.) The remaining states are known as equitable distribution states, where law specifies that it is up to the courts to divide the marital property equitably, taking into account such factors as the length of marriage, the age, health, and occupational skills of the parties, child-custody provisions, and property values. If you want to avoid having a divorce court divide your assets and decide your financial future, a prenuptial agreement can be a very efficient way of protecting yourself.

A prenuptial agreement is not necessary if both partners agree that their assets will be governed by the laws of their state if they divorce or separate. But for those who have accumulated considerable separate assets, or who have children by a previous marriage whom they wish to protect financially, a premarital agreement is advisable. Such an agreement will also help define how jointly owned assets will be split and how separate assets will be treated in the event of a divorce, regardless of the laws of the state in which you are living at the time you are married or divorced. The agreement will also let you define how your respective incomes are split during the marriage and upon divorce.

AND BABY MAKES THREE
(OR SOMETIMES TWO)

CHILD-CARE EXPENSES

◇ The problem of child care confronts almost every working mother. If you pay someone to take care of your child outside your home, either individually or in a group setting, you are not required to pay Social Security taxes on your payments. But if you employ someone in your home to take care of your children, you are responsible for Social Security tax on the caretaker's salary if you pay her more than $50 per quarter. You may withhold one-half of the Social Security tax from your employee's pay, or you may agree to pay the entire tax yourself. After you file Form SS-4 with the Internal Revenue Service, you will be assigned an employer identification number and you will begin receiving quarterly Forms 942 to file.

CHILD-CARE CREDIT

◇ If you are working, looking for a job, or attending school full time, you are entitled to claim a credit on your federal tax return for qualifying child- and dependent-care expenses. The expenses must be for children who are under 13 years of age, and the credit is figured as a percentage of your expenses. The maximum amount of expenses that qualify are $2,400 per year for one child and $4,800 for two or more children, and the credit works on a sliding scale ranging from 30 percent of your qualified expenses if your income is below $10,000, to 20 percent of your expenses if your income exceeds $28,000. You must be able to identify the individual or organization that provides the care.

YOUR CHILDREN'S EDUCATIONAL EXPENSES

◇ The cost of education has been growing faster than general inflation, and it is generally agreed that at least a 6 to 7 percent annual increase in education costs is probable for the next 10 years. These figures mean that by the time your newborn is ready for college, costs will have tripled.

Accumulating a college fund that is adequate to support the entire cost of your children's education may not be possible. Part of the cost will be squeezed out of your monthly budget, your child may need to work part-time while in school, and scholarships and student loans may make up the difference. What you can do now is to establish a custodial account in your child's name. By doing so, you can save taxes as you save for your child's education. Children under 14 are allowed to earn $550 a year of investment income tax-free. The next $550 is taxed at the child's tax rate, and additional earnings are taxed at the parents' tax rate. Children 14 and older pay tax at their own tax rates, generally 15 percent.

If your 14-year-old earns $2,500 a year in interest income, the tax will be $375. If you had kept the investments in your own name, and you are in the 31 percent tax bracket, you would owe tax of $775; by putting the investments in your child's name, you have saved $400 in taxes. If your child is under 14, the tax would be $540, still $235 less than you would pay on the income.

Custodial accounts are easy to establish, but beware of the pitfalls. Once you transfer money into the account, you cannot withdraw it for your own purposes, nor can you use it to pay expenses you are legally required to furnish for your child, such as food, housing, and clothing. When your child reaches the age of majority, generally 18 or 21, depending on the laws of the state in which you live, the money in the account may be legally withdrawn by your child. You may hope that your child will spend the money on education, but you cannot legally require it. If you want to put money in your child's name but you fear what your child will do with the money at age 18, you may set up a Crummey trust, which is more elaborate than a custodial account. Under a Crummey trust, your child is given a window of opportunity to withdraw the accrued money at the age of majority. If your child does not exercise that option, the money will remain subject to the trust provisions for payout at a future date.

If you buy Series EE savings bonds in your own name and use the money to pay your children's tuition bills, you will escape tax on the interest if your income in the year you cash the bonds is less than $41,900 ($62,900 for a married couple). Some of the income will be excludable if your other income is more than $41,900, but not more than $57,700 ($94,350 for a married couple).

YOUR CHILD'S TAX RETURN

◇ Your child is required to file a tax return if his total income exceeds $3,600, or if his unearned income, such as from interest and dividends, is $550 or more. If your child is under 14, you may include his or her income on a special form that you attach to your tax return, and pay the child's taxes along with your own. Children under the age of 14 pay tax on unearned income at a higher rate than older children and adults, so if your child is under the age of 14 and is earning more than $1,100 from investments, consider such tax-deferred investments as U.S. savings bonds. The earnings will not be taxed until the bonds mature, and if the child is 14 or older when that occurs, they will be taxed at the child's lower rate. Other investments appropriate for children under 14 are growth stocks and municipal bonds.

MARRIAGE AND YOUR CREDIT

It is very important to maintain credit in your own name after you are married. If you don't maintain your own credit, your credit cards may be canceled if you are widowed or divorced. If you are married and do not have credit cards, apply for one in your own name now. If you are told that you need a co-signer, get a co-signer other than your husband, such as a parent, sibling, or friend, so that the credit will be yours and not your husband's. (See chapter 7 for details about establishing credit if you are divorced or widowed.)

In an equitable distribution state that recognizes separate property, your husband's co-signature is not required on a credit application. In a community property state, where income and property are considered to belong equally to both spouses, it is legal for the credit institution to collect information about your spouse, but they cannot require his co-signature. The law allows a creditor to request information concerning your spouse if you reside in a community property state, if your spouse will be contractually liable for the account, or if you are relying on his income as a basis for repayment of the debt. But even though you may have to give information about your spouse, if you live in a community property state you do not have to get your husband to co-sign the loan if half of your community property and income will qualify you for the loan.

If you are borrowing money that will be secured by property owned jointly by both of you, or as community property, the creditor may ask for your husband's signature on the mortgage or deed of trust, even if you will be solely responsible for repayment. The creditor may not ask for your husband's signature on the bank note unless he is going to be specifically obligated to repay the debt.

Even if you have not applied for credit in your own name, your credit history will reflect all accounts on which you are an authorized user. Since 1977, all accounts must be reported in both spouses' names if they both use the account or if they are both contractually obligated to repay the debt. This can work for you or against you, depending on whether your mate is fiscally responsible. If you are divorced and your ex-spouse had a bad credit history, you may be able to disassociate yourself from his credit record by attaching a note to your credit application explaining the situation, and by placing a statement of 100 words or less in your credit file (see chapter 2). By law, a creditor must consider any information that you present to indicate that your credit report does not accurately reflect your creditworthiness.

MARRIAGE AND BANKRUPTCY

If you are married and your husband declares bankruptcy, you will probably be forced into bankruptcy as well, particularly if you live in a state with community property laws. If you live in an equitable distribution state, investigate whether it is possible for you to avoid bankruptcy when your husband files. In the event that you are in the process of divorce when he files for bankruptcy, your divorce proceedings will probably be halted until the bankruptcy proceedings are complete, and your attorney may advise you to join with your husband in filing for bankruptcy. If the divorce is complete before your husband files for bankruptcy, you may not be dragged into bankruptcy yourself. However, if your financial situation is such that your debts will force you into bankruptcy, it probably will be cheaper for you and your husband to file jointly for bankruptcy before you complete your divorce proceedings. (See chapter 2 for a description of the process for declaring bankruptcy.)

4

INVESTING FOR YOUR FUTURE

ESTABLISHING FINANCIAL GOALS

The key to sound financial planning is goal setting. Since "goals" is merely an abstract term for wants and needs, in order to reach your goals, you simply work to satisfy your wants and needs, giving up the things that have no real importance to you and focusing on those that do. Although it is simple in concept, financial goal setting takes patience, perseverance, and a good deal of introspection. With a little effort, however, you can soon be well on the way to creating and achieving your financial goals.

To begin, make two lists: One of things you want, and a second of things you need. List as many goals as you can think of, including both short-term and long-term ambitions. Now pick out one-third of the items on your list as the goals on which you would most like to concentrate. For each of these items, list ways that you can begin now to satisfy that goal.

For example, if you want a new home, you first need a down payment. Under your goal of a new home write "down payment," and the amount you will need. (The down payment required will be at least 10 to 20 percent of the purchase price.) Under that amount, list what you can do now to begin setting aside that down payment. "Save $200 per month" might be appropriate. "Get a part-time job" might be another solution, and "cash savings bonds" or "borrow from parents" are other possible options.

As you focus on listing your goals, choose those that seem reasonably achievable, but don't limit yourself in listing what comes to mind. Then figure out what you really want and when you would like to have it. A real commitment to the goals you have set will help you overcome obstacles you may encounter as you strive to reach those goals.

Using the goals from your needs and wants list, prepare a goals worksheet, indicating how important the goal is to you, when you would like to achieve it, and how much it will take to fulfill that goal in today's dollars. (See Appendix A.)

Once you have identified your goals and have set a general timetable for reaching them, as well as noting the amount you will need to attain them in today's dollars, it is time to create objectives. This means deciding how much you need to save each month to achieve each goal, where those savings will come from, and how they will be invested. Take a separate piece of paper for each item on your list, and then be specific about this information for each goal. (See Appendix B.)

INVESTING

THE THREE CATEGORIES OF INVESTMENT

◇ Now it is time to invest your savings. Some people fail to save because they simply don't know what to do with their money. Without guidance, investment possibilities can seem both endless and confusing. But this is only an illusion, for there are really only three major areas in which to invest: cash, financial assets, and "real" assets. Cash includes the money in your wallet and the proceeds of your checking accounts, savings accounts, money market accounts, short-term certificates of deposit, and Treasury bills. Financial assets fall into two categories: stocks, through which you become a shareholder in a company; and bonds, through which you loan money to a company, government, or municipality. "Real" assets are tangible and include real estate, oil and gas, and antiques. Every investment fits into these general categories, and your investment portfolio eventually will include holdings in each of these groups.

Cash and cash equivalents provide liquidity, which means they can be converted to cash when needed, and they produce good income when interest rates are high. Cash is also a category in which to park your money while waiting for the right investment to come along. When opportunity knocks, your investment funds will be available.

In the category of financial assets, bonds provide continuing income. They vary in safety, however, from ultra-safe U.S. Treasury obligations to the high-risk junk bonds that were the downfall of many investors of the recent past. Time also increases the riskiness of bonds: short-term bonds pose very little risk of price fluctuation, but long-term bonds bear a great deal of market risk. Like the sway of a skyscraper in a hurricane or an earthquake, one may not feel the movement on the ground floor, but as you go higher the sway becomes greater.

Most financial assets are at their performance peak in times of low inflation and low interest rates. Like bonds, some stocks are riskier than others. Blue-chip and dividend-paying stocks are the least risky, and high-flying technology growth stocks and new issues are among the riskiest. Income from stocks varies as well: those paying high dividends often show little growth, while growth stocks pay no or minimal dividends but have a high potential for appreciation.

Real estate is often appealing because one can actually see and touch it, hence its categorization as a "real" asset. Real estate has potential for appreciation, and rental real estate has an income stream that can be sheltered from immediate taxes by depreciation write-offs. But real estate is among the most illiquid of investments. Although it tends to increase in value in times of high inflation and high interest rates, it is also difficult to sell during these periods, as buyers are reluctant to borrow mortgage money at high interest rates. Real estate has other risks as well, such as risk of local economic slowing or recession, resulting in poor rental markets, little or no appreciation, or actual depreciation. While real estate has many benefits, the risks are, nevertheless, substantial.

To control investment risk, a sound financial portfolio must be balanced among the investments available. Every investment has certain risks, and the various risks of different investments can be used to offset each other. For example, as interest rates climb, money market interest rates increase, but the value of long-term bonds you already own declines.

And so it goes. Every investment is risky in one way or another, but by balancing your portfolio, you can create strength from these risks. In general, the riskier an investment, the higher the potential reward. By balancing the risks, you can reap higher rewards without subjecting your portfolio to undue loss. Risk is therefore a variable over which you can exert some control through strategic investing.

A BRIEF SURVEY OF INVESTMENT MODES

Here are some of the investments that fit the major investment modes.

Defensive investments	Savings accounts
	Money market accounts
	Treasury bills
	Short-term certificates of deposit
	Short-term bonds
Conservative investments	Intermediate-term bonds and CDs
	Government National Mortgage Association (GNMA) funds
	High-yield stocks
	Fixed annuities
Moderate investments	Long-term bonds
	Growth stocks
	Variable annuities
	Low-leverage real estate

	Producing oil and gas well investments
Aggressive—and riskier— investments	Junk bonds
	Options
	High-leverage real estate
	Oil-drilling funds
	Precious metals
	Collectibles
Daredevil investments (Not recommended for most people)	Penny stocks
	Venture capital
	Raw land and development
	Wildcat drilling
	Precious gems
	Commodities futures

STAY-ing Power

◇ To invest strategically, you must develop a working perspective about investments and their attributes. Investments, in general, can be said to reflect four basic attributes that are easy to recall because their first letters combine to spell "STAY." They are Safety, Tax savings, Appreciation, and Yield. No investments have all four attributes, and most investments have only one or two, but a prudent combination of the attributes will keep your investment portfolio healthy and thriving.

An investment in a money market account, for example, will give you yield and safety. For appreciation and tax benefits, real estate with a low mortgage balance ("low-leverage") fills the bill. Its current income is sheltered from taxation by depreciation write-offs, and real estate has potential for long-term appreciation. When interest rates and inflation are low, an investment in common stocks is wise. A growth mutual fund will give you the greatest appreciation, but supplies less current income. If income is important to you, an income or bond fund will fit your needs. Or perhaps a balanced mutual fund invested for both growth and income will be best for you.

Building a portfolio of investments, and then managing it, is no more complicated than managing your nutritional needs. Even the concepts are similar: The various food groups (investments) are combined to supply the nutritional needs (growth and income) and individual tastes (risk tolerance and investment philosophies) of the individual (investor), while staying within one's budget (portfolio size). The difference is that we are taught the four major food groups and how they combine to create a balanced diet when we are in elementary school, but most people are never taught how investments can interlock to provide growth, income, and stability.

In creating a portfolio, your stage of life, your family situation, and the time frame in which you make your investments are major factors in determining your liquidity needs, your diversification requirements, and your risk tolerance. The purpose is to create a portfolio of investments that will allow you the greatest possible confidence as you take maximum advantage of investment returns.

To determine what investment combination is right for your portfolio, first consider "STAY-ing Power." Do so by assigning a total of 10 points to all 4 factors—Safety, Tax benefits, Appreciation, and Yield—but assign no more than 4 points to any single factor. For example, one 30-year-old married woman with a small child and a lucrative career assigned points as follows:

Safety	2 points
Tax benefits	4 points
Appreciation	4 points
Yield	0 points
Total	10 points

This woman seeks tax benefits, since she is in a high tax bracket, and appreciation, since she is saving for a new home and investing both for her child's education and her own retirement. Safety is not a great concern, as she could regenerate possible investment losses through her earnings. Because she needs no additional income, current yield is of no concern to her.

Another woman, age 70, single, retired, and in good health, made this allocation:

Safety	4 points
Tax benefits	0 points
Appreciation	2 points
Yield	4 points
Total	10 points

She is concerned about the safety of her investments; because she is retired, she can't afford any loss of her investment capital. And since investments provide most of her retirement income, she wants high current yield. Her tax bracket is low, so tax benefits don't concern her. She recognizes appreciation as a factor, but not a large one: She needs her nest egg to keep pace with inflation, but nothing more.

As you select particular investments for your portfolio, the factors of liquidity, diversification, time frame, and risk tolerance come into play. The 30-year-old woman needs the down payment for a new house in 5 years, so a 5-year U.S. Treasury bond will suit her portfolio better than a 30-year bond. The 70-year-old woman has no imminent need for large sums of cash, so she might seek the higher yields of a 30-year bond. Since she is likely to die before the bond matures, she will be assured the higher income for life.

Other factors come into play as well, of course. The older woman remembers the Depression, and she has always shied away from stocks as a result. The stock market crash of 1987 did nothing to increase her confidence in the stock market, and although her financial adviser recommended that she invest 25 percent of her money in high-grade stocks, she is still leery of the stock market. Consequently, in her case, diversification must give way to her particular capacity for risk tolerance. After a long discussion about the risks of inflation, she decided to invest some money in utility-company stocks. After all, she reasoned, everyone uses utilities, and the utility rates certainly keep going up. She decided to invest 30 percent of her funds in U.S. government bonds, 20 percent in bank certificates of deposit, 10 percent in international bonds, 15 percent in utility stocks, 10 percent in a money market account, and 15 percent in real estate, all through mutual funds, investment entities that pool investors' money under professional management.

The younger woman has invested 20 percent of her funds in U.S.

government bonds, 40 percent in growth stocks, 20 percent in real estate, 10 percent in international stocks, and 10 percent in a tax-free money market account. Since she is a busy professional, she used mutual funds as the instrument for all her investments.

REBALANCING YOUR PORTFOLIO

◇ Periodically, both women should rebalance their portfolios, bringing them back to their original percentages. Here, for example, is the value of the 30-year-old's portfolio a year after her original investment:

	ORIGINALLY		ONE YEAR LATER	
U.S. bonds	20%	$10,000	16%	$9,000
Growth stock	40%	$20,000	43%	$24,000
Real estate	20%	$10,000	22%	$12,000
International stocks	10%	$5,000	9%	$5,000
Money market	10%	$5,000	10%	$5,500
Total	100%	$50,000	100%	$55,500

To rebalance her portfolio, she should sell $1,800 of the growth stock fund and $900 of the real estate fund, investing $2,100 in the bond fund, $550 in the international stock fund, and $50 in the money market account. By rebalancing her portfolio, she will be selling investments that have increased in value and investing the proceeds in assets that have decreased in value. She is selling high and buying low, the classic investment strategy, and she is maintaining a portfolio that is balanced for risk, therefore protecting her investments in bad times as well as good. This strategy improves the long-term performance of her investment portfolio so that her money is working at the same time that she is.

Smart investors manage their portfolios wisely. They invest for the long term, rebalancing their investments periodically and adjusting asset mixes as their financial goals change. Using STAY-ing Power to tame risk, they create high-performance portfolios that stay productive with minimum effort. By taming risk, they also harness its energy, and their net worth reaps the rewards.

MUTUAL FUNDS

◇ We have noted how important diversification is within investment categories, and one way of achieving that diversification with reduced risk is by investing in mutual funds. Mutual funds are private enterprises that pool investors' money under professional management to buy a portfolio of investments in one or more investment categories. Almost every type of investment can be bought through mutual funds.

In 1992 there are more than 3,300 funds with 62 million shareholders and $1.2 trillion under management. One-fourth of all American households, and more than one-third of *Consumer Reports* readers, own stock or bond mutual funds. The popularity of mutual funds is well deserved, for they offer the kind of full-time professional management and informed diversification that would be otherwise impossible to attain in a small investment portfolio. A good method to use when investing in mutual funds is known as dollar-cost averaging, which means investing a fixed amount in a mutual fund every month, for example, no matter what the current status of either the stock market or of current interest rates. In months when the price of your mutual fund is down, you will be able to buy more shares with your dollars than in months when the price is up. Through dollar-cost averaging, your shares will cost less on average than if you bought them all at once. And dollar-cost averaging also will create a sensible regular savings habit.

Mutual funds fall into a wide range of categories. Your choice will depend upon your investment goals and your tolerance for risk.

Aggressive growth. These funds strive for large gains by investing in small companies or highly volatile stocks.
Growth. Growth funds seek long-term capital gains through investment in companies that are growing faster than inflation.
Growth and income. While these funds emphasize growth, they

also concentrate on capital preservation through deriving income from current dividends.

Income. Income funds invest in high-yield stocks, preferred stock, and bonds to produce income.

Balanced. These funds invest in a combination of stocks and bonds to minimize risk.

Global and international. As the name indicates, these funds invest in international stocks or bonds to obtain global diversification and higher returns when the dollar is falling.

Specialty and sector. These funds invest in stocks of companies in a particular field or sector of the economy, such as health, utilities, oil, et cetera.

Corporate bonds. Corporate bond funds generally invest in the bonds of highly rated corporations.

Municipal bonds. These funds invest in bonds that are issued by states and municipalities, most often to fund public projects such as bridges and highways.

Government securities. U.S. government bond funds invest in U.S. Treasury and other bonds issued by government agencies.

Money market. Also called money funds, these invest in short-term Treasury bills, commercial paper, certificates of deposit, et cetera.

The income you earn from your mutual fund will be reduced by investment expenses, which include management fees and other expenses. In addition, certain mutual funds charge a sales commission called a "load." This commission, which ranges from 2 percent to 8.5 percent of the amount you invest, is generally paid to the stockbroker or financial planner who sold you the fund. While a stockbroker or financial planner can sometimes be useful in helping a novice choose mutual funds, if you wish to make your own decisions, consider investing in those funds that do not charge a sales commission, called "no-load" funds. These funds are not available through most stockbrokers; you buy them directly from the mutual fund company. Most money management magazines periodically publish performance surveys of major mutual funds, and these surveys usually include pertinent data for the fund, including fund type, fund performance, the minimum investment required, and a telephone number you can call to request a prospectus for the fund.

The prospectus is a fund document that contains the information that the Securities and Exchange Commission (SEC) requires to be furnished to you before you invest. It includes the fund's objectives and policies, the services it offers, the names of its officers and directors, its methods of purchasing and redeeming shares, the amount of its sales charges and management fees, and its financial statements.

Here is what to look for as you review a mutual fund's prospectus:

1. *Investment objective.* This section will tell you the objectives of the fund—whether it seeks income, growth, or undervalued stocks, for example. It will also note whether the fund is required to be fully invested in stocks, or if it can move in and out of the market as conditions fluctuate. For bond funds, the prospectus will indicate the average maturity of the underlying bonds.
2. *Past performance.* The prospectus supplies five years of operating results in a table of per-share income and capital changes. It also gives the ratio of its expenses to net assets (usually about 1 percent), and its portfolio turnover rate. Its total return is not required to be disclosed, but this will appear in the fund's annual report, which you can request.
3. *Management.* This is an optional section, but it usually lists the names and qualifications of the portfolio managers.
4. *Miscellaneous.* The back pages of the prospectus explain exchange privileges between funds in that family of funds, how to make withdrawals from the fund, et cetera.

Here are the questions to ask as you read a mutual fund prospectus:

1. Does this fund match my goals?
2. How much latitude does the fund have to switch in and out of markets?
3. Can the fund borrow money to increase its investments?

4. What is the fund's long-term track record?

5. How does the fund's performance compare with the S&P (Standard & Poor's) 500-stock index or with the fund records available in various investor magazines?

6. Has there been a continuity of management and investment objectives?

7. How big is the fund? For a growth fund, $50 million to $500 million is best. If the fund is any bigger than that, the manager is trying to steer the Queen Mary and may have trouble locating enough stocks or other investment instruments that satisfy the growth criteria.

8. Does the fund charge a sales commission (load)? If so, is it front-load (commission deducted from the money you invest), back-load (commission deducted from sales proceeds), or inside-load (commission deducted from fund earnings over a number of years)? What other fees are involved?

9. Are commissions charged on reinvested dividends? Avoid funds that do this.

10. What is the ratio of the fund's expenses to its net assets?

11. Are red flags—such as pending lawsuits or regulatory reviews—in evidence?

12. Read the risk clause in the prospectus, which will note the circumstances under which you can lose the money you invest in it. A good rule of thumb: The longer the clause, the riskier the investment.

In choosing bond funds, you must decide between a taxable mutual fund or a nontaxable municipal bond fund, which may be specific to the state where you live. To compare the two, subtract your tax bracket from 100 percent. For example, if you are in a 31 percent tax bracket, you will subtract 31 percent from 100 percent, which is 69 percent. Now divide the tax-free yield by that number and the result is the equivalent taxable yield. For example, a 6 percent tax-free yield on a municipal bond is the equivalent of an 8.7 percent taxable yield on a U.S. Treasury bond to someone in a 31 percent bracket. This means that a taxable bond fund paying 9 percent or more has an investment yield superior to that of a tax-free municipal bond fund paying 6 percent.

When you select a mutual fund, avoid these common traps.

Trap #1: The latest rage. Don't pick a fund because it's attracting a lot of excited publicity or because it's new. Look instead for a mutual fund with a proven track record.

Trap #2: Recent performance. Don't pick a fund simply because it did well recently; find one that has done well over 5 to 10 years, in all kinds of investment weather.

Trap #3: Cumulative returns. Even cumulative returns over a period of time do not tell you about the consistency of the fund's returns. For example, if you invest in a fund with high cumulative returns but great volatility, you could lose money. If the fund lost 40 percent the first year, then made 67 percent the next, you would merely break even, despite the 13.5 percent average gain noted overall for the two-year period.

ANNUITIES

◇ An annuity can be an efficient way of accumulating money for some people. In the category known as an immediate annuity, you deposit a lump sum with an insurance company or other financial institution, which, in turn, agrees to make payments to you for life, beginning immediately. A portion of each payment you receive is considered to be a return of your investment and is not taxable. This type of annuity is most commonly purchased by the retired or soon-to-be retired.

A deferred annuity is used to accumulate funds to be paid to you in the future. When you purchase a deferred annuity, your premium is invested on your behalf until future notice, and you pay no tax on those earnings until you withdraw the funds, either in a lump sum or in monthly payments.

Deferred annuities come in two basic forms: fixed and variable.

Fixed annuities guarantee a specified rate of return each year. Once your annuity begins payments to you, you will receive a fixed monthly payment, either for life or for another fixed period. You can also choose an option called "life and period certain," which guarantees payments to you for life; if you die early, your designated beneficiary will receive payments for the remainder of the guarantee period, which is usually 10 or 20 years. You may also opt for a joint-and-survivor life annuity, which continues paying each month until the death of the last to die of the two annuitants. If you choose a variable annuity, you may opt to invest your funds in a variety of mutual funds as well as a guaranteed income account, and the monthly payments you receive will vary according to the investment results of your capital. Under a variable annuity, the payment might increase over the years, helping combat the damage done by inflation.

When you purchase a deferred annuity, you need not specify the payout option at the beginning of the contract period. A deferred annuity, like an immediate annuity, is only as safe as the company that issued it. Although the funds you invest in variable annuity mutual funds are sequestered, the guarantee of fixed annuities depends on the health of the insurance company. So if you invest in fixed annuities rather than in variable ones, be sure you invest only with A+ rated companies (consult Best's Insurance Reports at your local library), particularly if you live in Washington, D.C., or one of the nine states (Alaska, Arkansas, California, Colorado, Louisiana, New Jersey, Ohio, South Dakota, or Wyoming) that do not have guaranty associations to cover contracts issued by bankrupt insurers.

The tax benefits are similar to those realized with an IRA, since the tax on earnings is deferred until you begin to receive the income, but unlike an IRA, payments to a deferred annuity are never tax-deductible.

If you are interested in an annuity, be sure to investigate the following features carefully:

- the current financial strength and track record of the insurance company issuing the contract
- the current interest rate and guarantee period for a fixed annuity, and the insurance company's record of investment results for a variable annuity

- the minimum guaranteed rate of interest and principal guarantees
- the presence of bailout provisions that allow you to surrender the contract without penalty if the interest rate falls below a specified amount
- the amount that you can withdraw from the contract each year without being subject to withdrawal charges imposed by the insurance company (note that any withdrawals before age 59½ are subject to IRS penalties of 10 percent)
- surrender charges, the period for which they apply, and the circumstances under which they are waived (death, disability, or annuity payout)

If you are married, and you die before you begin to take payments from your deferred annuity, your spouse may continue the deferred annuity. But if your beneficiary is not your spouse, he or she must begin taking payments within five years of your death, either through a lump-sum distribution or by way of periodic payments, and also must pay income tax on a portion of the proceeds. If you have already started receiving payments at the time of your death, the payments to the beneficiary will depend on the options you picked when you began to receive payments.

FINDING FINANCIAL GUIDANCE

◇ If you find you need financial guidance, you can obtain it from many sources. A number of professionals are trained to provide financial guidance. Your tax accountant can offer specific guidance on structuring your investments and other holdings so as to minimize income taxes. An estate attorney can draw up wills and trusts that will reduce the taxes on your estate when you die. Your insurance agent can assess your insurance needs. A fee-based financial adviser can help you define your goals and investment preferences and assist you in creating a strategic plan for money management. A stockbroker or commission-based financial adviser can implement that plan, or you can turn to a fee-only money manager to supervise your investments. Or, you can take a more active role in your financial planning and place your money in the kinds of mutual funds described earlier, based on their past performance and your current needs.

Some financial advisers have a vested interest in selling you products that will earn them commissions, and that may not be in your best interests. To find a competent and trustworthy financial adviser, ask friends, family members, or colleagues in your general financial situation for their recommendations, then interview those advisers to see how well their style meshes with yours.

INTERVIEWING FINANCIAL ADVISERS

◇ When you interview a prospective financial adviser, these questions will help you elicit the information you need to select the right one:

1. *What services will you provide?* If you need help with goal setting or retirement planning, you need an adviser who works in these areas, not a specialized money manager.

2. *What kinds of clients and size of accounts do you handle?* You are looking for an adviser who is familiar with your type of situation and who will give you the service you deserve. Your portfolio should fit neatly into the adviser's account range. In particular, you want to avoid an adviser who generally handles much larger portfolios and who, therefore, might consider yours unworthy of careful attention.

3. *What types of investments do you generally recommend?* If you are looking for a full range of investment products, don't choose an adviser who recommends only bonds. Press this question until you are clear about the adviser's preferences.

4. *Do you handle your clients' assets directly?* Be wary of financial advisers who want you to hand over all your investment assets.

5. *What is the financial planning process you use, and with whom will I work?* Your adviser should be able to explain his or her techniques for guiding you to investments that suit your needs. Your investment plan should be customized to your particular situation, and there should be one person

whom you trust who will be primarily responsible for your account and with whom you will have personal contact.

6. *How are you compensated?* The adviser may be paid an hourly fee, a percent of capital managed, or a flat fee. Some advisers are not compensated until you invest, and then they receive commissions on the investments they recommend. Other advisers receive a portion of their compensation from fees and the rest from commissions. Frequently, such advisers will offset the fees they charge you by commissions they earn on the investment products they sell you. Note that advisers who receive commissions have an obvious incentive to sell you financial products.

7. *Will you furnish references?* Ask for the names and telephone numbers of the adviser's clients whose situations are similar to yours and who have been clients for several years. Telephone those references and ask about the adviser's investment performance and service.

YOUR NEW HOME: TO RENT OR TO BUY?

When you look for new housing, you must decide whether to rent or buy. Though home ownership is the American Dream, it may not be the best financial choice for you, and you will want to consider carefully the differences that owning versus renting will make in your own particular financial plan. Owning your own home gives you tax write-offs in the form of deductible interest and property taxes. This means that your income taxes could be reduced by as much as one-third of your real estate taxes and mortgage interest. The amount of tax savings depends on your tax bracket. Consider that if your house payment were $1,000 per month, which is mostly deductible, then after your tax savings you would be out of pocket each month only $700 or so. If you could rent a similar house for $600, then renting for $600 instead of owning for $700 appears to be a better deal.

Of course, if you rent rather than own, you won't enjoy the

appreciation that takes place as your home increases in value. But what if you live in an area where housing prices are going down rather than up? While the price for a single-family home has generally increased at about 2 percent above the rate of inflation over the past 25 years, in some areas it was higher and in other areas lower, and in some years prices rose dramatically while in other years they plunged. Although investing in your own home is generally a good hedge against inflation, during a housing slump, which can last for years, renting is often your best bet. In a slow real estate market, many rental properties are available to choose from, since property owners who can't find buyers at the right price often will rent their property and wait out the market slowdown. If you are considering the purchase of a home in a slow market, renting can give you an opportunity to test drive the house at a lower cost. When you sense that the market is turning around, this might be a good time to make your landlord an offer on the house. If the owner can save real estate commissions by selling directly to you, these savings might then be passed on to you in the form of a purchase price lower than if a broker were to be involved.

The benefits of renting:

- no down payment required
- few maintenance costs
- no long-term commitment to a particular property or location
- in a poor real estate market, the ability to save money by renting at a bargain rate

The drawbacks of renting:

- inability to take advantage of the tax benefits available to homeowners, who can deduct their property taxes and interest
- vulnerability to rent increases
- more restrictions and less privacy than in a property you own
- the possibility of being evicted if you fall behind in your pay-

ments, as opposed to having longer to catch up and avoid fore-closure if you own the property

WHAT YOU CAN AFFORD

◇ If you decide to buy a home, you must find the right one for your needs at the proper price, and you must also arrange for the financing. Before you can begin to look, you need to determine how much you can afford in monthly payments and how much of a down payment you can make.

To determine the purchase price you can afford, a good rule of thumb is that your housing costs, which include taxes and insurance, should not exceed 28 percent of your gross monthly income, and your total debt should not exceed 36 percent. Lending institutions will allow you to make a down payment of only 10 percent, but it's best to plan on making a down payment of at least 20 percent of the purchase price of your new home so that you need not buy mortgage insurance, which generally costs about .25 percent of the loan amount.

For example, if you earn $4,000 a month, your housing costs should not exceed 28 percent of that amount, or $1,120 a month. Multiply that $1,120 by 100, and you will find that you can afford a mortgage of approximately $112,000. If you purchase a $140,000 home and put 20 percent down, the down payment required would be $28,000. While this method will give you a general idea of how expensive a house you can afford, it's best to consult your lending institution to obtain a more accurate number, which will be based on lending conditions in your particular area and on prevailing interest rates.

Shop for the financing for your new home before you shop for the house itself. If a lender will prequalify you for a loan, you may be able to purchase property at a lower price, since the seller will know that you will be able to close on the home rapidly. This prequalification can be a valuable negotiating point for you. In addition, by knowing how much of a loan you qualify for, you will ensure that you are shopping in the right price range when you look for a new home, rather than being surprised by a bank's mortgage policies when you are under pressure to move forward and secure your purchase.

HOUSING ALTERNATIVES

◇ The variety of homes available today includes houses, condominiums, town houses, cooperatives, and mobile homes. When you purchase a condominium, a town house, and certain other attached dwellings, you hold title to the unit you own and share with other owners a proportional ownership in the property's common areas and amenities. You pay a monthly maintenance fee to the homeowners' association, which pays for maintenance, insurance, and taxes on the common grounds. If you buy a cooperative, you own a share of stock in the corporation that owns the cooperative building, and the co-op gives you the right to use your apartment and the common areas. Your approval by the co-op's board of directors is often required, in which case you will have to submit financial statements and personal references and attend an interview.

Be certain to investigate carefully when you are considering the purchase of this kind of housing. Have the shareholders or other owners been subjected to recent additional assessments for necessary repairs or renovation? Are more such assessments contemplated? Does the property's developer still own shares in the condo or co-op? If so, what is that developer's own financial condition? Does the property have a reserve fund sufficient to deal with anticipated capital improvements, or will the property owners be responsible? The importance of your retaining a real estate attorney who specializes in representing buyers of these property types cannot be emphasized enough.

Condominiums, town houses, and mobile homes are generally less expensive than other types of housing and may seem to be the best alternative for you. But remember that in a housing slowdown, condominiums and town houses often lose value and are more difficult to sell than independently owned houses. That is in part because the association fee or other regular maintenance cost is a fixed amount that is considered by a potential buyer as an integral part of the purchase price. In a poor market, as potential buyers compare the monthly cost of your condominium or co-op with another seller's house, they will be willing to pay relatively less for your condominium or town house as they work to equalize the relative costs. As house prices fall, they will be willing to pay less and less, and all of the decrease will come from your condominium's or co-op's sale price, as the condo, maintenance, or association fee will not change.

Mobile homes are popular and economical, but they have drawbacks as well. Most mobile-home owners do not own the pad on which the mobile home sits, but rather rent it from a mobile-home park, and the pad rental is subject to periodic rent increases. In addition, mobile-home construction is not of the same permanent nature as that of a house, and mobile homes therefore eventually wear out, much like cars. In addition, the cost of heating and cooling a mobile home may be considerably more than the cost of heating or cooling a similarly sized house. Even with these drawbacks, mobile homes are an attractively priced housing alternative. Be certain, however, to interview others in the park you are considering to determine their experience on the site.

SHOPPING FOR A HOME

◇ The more you know about your price range, your tastes, and your housing needs, the easier it will be to communicate those needs to a real estate agent and to find the best property at the proper price. Follow the classified ads in your local newspaper, visit real estate open houses, and let brokers know what kind of housing you are seeking.

You may find a bargain if you locate a seller who is anxious to wrap up a sale and will accept a lower price. Perhaps the seller's house has been on the market for a long time, or the house is already vacant. A seller who is divorcing or has recently experienced a death in the family may also be particularly eager to sell. Your real estate agent may be able to locate properties on which the lending institution has foreclosed, or ones that are about to go into foreclosure. A seller may be willing to transfer the property to you for the amount of existing debt rather than letting it go into foreclosure. But often the combination of home equity loans and declining real estate prices means that the property owner owes more on the property than it is currently worth. In that case, the owner is better off letting it go into foreclosure so that those debts are extinguished. Because the real estate broker's sales commission comes from the purchase price, he or she may advise you to make a higher offer than the seller might be willing to settle for. Make your offers judiciously.

If possible, look for the home you will need tomorrow as well as today. It is not wise to buy a house that you are likely to outgrow shortly, nor is it wise to buy a house that will soon be too big for your needs. Select a house that you will be comfortable in for a number of years, one in which you can tally the appreciation while your house payment stays the same. Trading up into more expensive housing is usually costly in terms of acquisition and financing costs, as well as increased monthly mortgage payments and insurance and property taxes.

Utility costs have escalated considerably in recent years, and it is important to examine utility bills before you buy a house. A house may cost $10,000 less than another, resulting in $100 less in monthly mortgage payments, but it will be no bargain if it is an energy waster that consumes an additional $150 per month in utilities.

Before buying a home, hire a home inspector who is a member of the American Society of Home Inspectors to survey the structure, the roof, and the electrical, heating, and plumbing systems, as well as the property's general interior. Include a contingency clause in your contract that allows you to be released from the agreement if the inspection reveals defects, and also a contingency clause that the sale will be canceled and your deposit refunded if you are unable to obtain satisfactory financing within 120 days. (In a sellers' market, the owner may insist on as little as 60 days for this financing period.) Your contract should also state how prorations will be made for such costs as insurance, taxes, utilities, homeowners' fees, et cetera, and it should provide for your obtaining a termite inspection and title search to guarantee you clear title to the property. Specify, too, what items are included in the sale price, such as curtains, appliances, and blinds, so no misunderstandings about these take place at closing.

FINANCING YOUR HOME

◇ To finance your new home, you will probably borrow from a bank or other lending institution, a mortgage banker, or a credit union. You may use a mortgage broker to help you find a suitable loan, in which case she or he will be paid directly by the financial institution that provides the mortgage, and your only cost will be a small application fee. Find out if you are eligible to qualify for Veterans Administration (VA) loans and loans backed by your state housing finance agency, or those offered by the U.S. Department of Housing and Urban Development (HUD), which sometimes make money available for loans to low- or moderate-income borrowers, or to first-time home buyers. If you do not use a mortgage broker, consult several financial institutions to find out all possible details about what might be the best loan for you. Your real estate agent may have information about the current rates being charged by lending institutions in your area, but don't feel obligated to go to a lender your real estate agent suggests. Rates can vary widely, so be sure to investigate carefully.

If you plan to live in your new home for a long time, you will probably be wise to obtain a fixed-rate mortgage, the kind of loan on which the monthly payment never varies. A fixed-rate mortgage is particularly valuable if interest rates are low when you purchase. If interest rates are high or you expect to move within a few years, an adjustable-rate mortgage (ARM) may be your best bet. Choose an adjustable-rate mortgage only if the base rate is 2 to 3 percent lower than fixed rates and you do not plan to own the house for more than five years. If interest rates are high, an adjustable-rate mortgage may be advantageous until interest rates decline and you can refinance at a fixed rate. Ask lending institutions about conversion clauses that will allow you to convert an adjustable-rate mortgage to a fixed-rate mortgage later without paying additional closing costs and points.

With an adjustable-rate loan, the interest rate and monthly payment will be adjusted periodically. Adjustable-rate mortgages are offered with an initial bargain teaser rate, which rapidly escalates. You need to know not only the initial rate, but on what basis it will be adjusted and how often. Be sure the mortgage has a cap—that is, a ceiling or set rate above which it cannot rise—and project a situation in which, for one reason or another, you are forced to pay that rate for a sustained period of time. If you base your budget on the initial rate, you may be hard-pressed to make payments when your payment amount increases. You can estimate your monthly mortgage payments in the future by obtaining a mortgage payment table, available at bookstores or from some lending institutions, which shows payment amounts required for a range of mortgages at a range of interest rates.

With an adjustable-rate mortgage your monthly payments will increase when interest rates go up. If your monthly payment stays the same, you will have negative amortization, so that the amount you owe the financial institution increases—instead of decreasing—every year, because your monthly payments do not even pay the interest on the loan.

When you shop for interest rates pay attention to whether the lending institution requires the payment of points as well. Points are lenders' fees based on a percentage of the loan amount, which are paid up front, in advance, at closing. If you plan to stay in your new home for several years, it will be to your advantage to pay an extra point (1 percent) up front to get an interest rate that is .5 percent lower. But if you plan to be in your home only a couple of years, paying extra points for a lower rate may not be wise. Also note whether the bank requires a prepayment penalty in the event that you decide to pay off the mortgage earlier than you anticipated.

If you decide to stay in your existing home, it may be wise to review your existing expenditures and to consider refinancing, particularly if you have an adjustable-rate mortgage and intend to stay in your home for several more years.

Find out what the current qualifying standards are for mortgages in your locality, and how best you might satisfy a lender's requirements. Sometimes you can negotiate with a lender.

PAYING CASH FOR A HOME

◇ If you have enough money, you may want to pay cash for your home. By doing so, you will save the initial financing costs, and you will not have to pay monthly mortgage payments. Paying cash for a house is the equivalent of investing that amount of money at the prevailing mortgage rate. For example, if you have the ability to pay cash, and the prevailing interest rate is 10 percent, you must be able to get better than 10 percent combined income and growth on your investments for it to make sense to invest your money elsewhere rather than using it to purchase your home. By paying cash you will lose the benefits of your tax deduction for home mortgage interest, but the lost tax deduction is offset by the advantage of not having to pay tax on the interest your money would have earned. While paying cash for your home can give you a considerable amount of security, be sure you have enough money left after your home purchase to meet future needs and emergencies that might arise.

Even if you can't afford to pay cash for your home, if you can afford a relatively substantial monthly house payment, consider financing your new home over 15 years rather than 30 years. Your mortgage payment will be a few hundred dollars more each month, but in 15 years it will be paid off and the amount of interest will be less. Most loan agreements do not impose prepayment penalties, so if you have a 30-year loan and now find that you have additional money available, make extra principal payments on your mortgage each month, and you will pay it off over a much shorter time and save on the interest.

DIVORCE

Divorce ranks at the top of most lists of stressful life events. Because it requires extreme change at almost every level, it means reconsidering your expectations and reassessing your life goals.

Once the prospect of divorce becomes an actuality, it is imperative that you find out as soon as possible the details of what lies ahead. The law will work in your favor only if you learn your legal rights and how to protect them.

The financial aspects of divorce deal with three things: division of marital property, alimony, and child support.

To reach an equitable division of marital property (an equal division in community property states), the marital property is identified, valued, and then divided. Your attorney will tell you what constitutes marital property in your state and how to identify it, which may involve tracing to the source of original investments and down payments. Valuation of the property can be quite complex, and varies from state to state. In some states, intangibles such as goodwill, trademarks, and even college degrees are deemed to have value, and in other states they are not. Likewise, final division of the marital property between the spouses depends on the laws of your state.

Alimony is awarded in many states, though in some states it is not. Alimony awards depend on the relative economics of the parties, and judges also consider such factors as the longevity of the marriage and sometimes marital misbehavior. Child support is more clear-cut, since most states have now adopted federally mandated child support guidelines that take into account the earnings of both parties, the custody and visitation arrangements, and the children's needs.

PREPARING FOR DIVORCE

Take steps now to protect yourself in the event that your marriage terminates in divorce. Even if you and your husband have not separated, or if you are separated and are working on a reconciliation, consider visiting an attorney to discuss your situation. Consulting an attorney doesn't compel you to file for divorce, but if you do and you are knowledgeable and confident about your legal rights, you may be able to negotiate a reasonable financial settlement with your husband in advance of legal proceedings. Once you are fully schooled in the divorce process, you will be able to act effectively on your own behalf, instead of only reacting as the proceedings unfold.

There are many reasons why your husband may prefer to negotiate directly with you rather than with your lawyer. First, he needn't pay $100 to $250 an hour to talk with you, the fees that divorce lawyers commonly charge. Second, he may believe that he can persuade you to accept whatever financial arrangement is best for him. Assuming that you are not expert in the divorce laws of your state, he may hope you will settle for what he is willing to relinquish, rather than what the law allows. Even if you and your husband are able to negotiate a settlement, however, you will still need some legal assistance to assure that you get the financial arrangement you deserve.

Many women who are about to divorce find themselves facing the first major financial transaction of their lives. Because the process presents many pitfalls, and because its financial consequences can be so great, it's wise to be aware of the ways you can make it work best for you. Here is a checklist to assist you in case of divorce:

1. Consult an attorney about your legal rights as soon as you anticipate the possibility of divorce. Don't engage the same

attorney who has handled your husband's business affairs or one who may be similarly committed to him.

2. Write a narrative for the divorce attorney you engage, detailing the facts of your marriage: the date you began living together, the date you married, your children's birthdates, previous separations, when various assets were acquired, and the separate property either of you brought into the marriage or inherited.

3. Gather information about what you own and owe. You'll need copies of financial statements, tax returns, retirement plan documents, brokerage statements, and insurance policies.

4. Obtain detailed information on each retirement plan in which you or your husband have participated.

5. Begin to think about what assets you would like to keep if you divorce, and which you are willing to give up. Consult with your accountant about the potential tax consequences of various options, especially of keeping your house.

6. Get preliminary estimates of the value of property you own, and list the debts that you owe. Pay bills and credit cards from joint funds before you separate, so you don't become responsible for them later.

7. Note the contents of the safe-deposit box. Secure both keys, if possible, so that your husband will not be able to enter the box and remove valuable papers and possessions. If you do not have both keys and you are afraid your husband may strip the contents, you may wish to photograph the contents of the box or even remove them and place them in another box under your control.

8. Prepare a spending history for last year from your checkbooks and other spending records, so you can determine your future needs and decide where to cut back, if necessary.

9. Before you separate, use joint funds to make any needed repairs to your automobile and home, buy necessary clothing for yourself and your children, and secure whatever dental and medical treatment may be in order. If you wait

until after separation, these expenses may be yours alone, depending on the laws of your state.

10. Set aside cash reserves to use in the first few months after separation. Transfer your share of joint funds to your separate bank account.

11. If you have not already done so, apply for credit cards in your own name. If possible, obtain credit cards with check-writing privileges.

12. After separation, close any joint credit card accounts, take control of both cards issued on the accounts, and notify creditors that you will no longer be responsible for your husband's charges on the accounts.

13. Open a convenient post office box that you can use to receive your mail before you separate and while you are in the process of divorce.

14. Begin a "divorce notebook," in which you list all problems that have to do with the impending separation and divorce. Also list each step that you take in the divorce process, including a synopsis of all telephone calls and conferences with your attorney and accountant.

15. Divorce will be less ominous if you figure out the worst scenario that might confront you in the future and decide in advance how you might deal with it. Investigate personal, family, and community resources that may be available to you.

16. Explore your career options. Use the crisis of divorce to direct yourself into a more satisfying future.

17. After consulting with your attorney, begin discussions about divorce with your husband, as calmly as possible. Find out what financial issues he seems adamant about, and where he is willing to make concessions. This fact-finding will be helpful when you begin actual negotiations through your attorney.

18. Get a feel for the territory you will be crossing by reading current books about divorce (see "Recommended Reading," page 231), attending family-law court proceedings, and talking with family members or friends who have divorced recently.

19. Find a good therapist or support group to help you through the months ahead.

20. Planning for divorce is best done deliberately and slowly. Take your time and don't rush matters. Negotiating the best possible settlement should be your primary focus; isolate it from the emotional issues of the marriage.

FOCUS ON THE IMPORTANCE OF HAVING CASH ASSETS

◇ Money is important, and having cash buys power in the marketplace. When you divide property and income, each of you will have only half of what you had before, and in some states, even less. And when you divide the available cash, you will probably end up with nothing at all, because the divorce process itself is almost always enormously expensive. Divorce greatly increases cash needs: One of you usually moves out of the home you have been sharing, for example, and this alone means paying substantial costs for a new residence, such as the first and last month's rent and a rental deposit. Added to this are the attorney's retainers, counseling fees, and duplicate living costs you probably will be paying. If you don't have your own regular income, you will need money to live on until you can obtain an award of alimony and child support, and you will need a cash reserve in case your husband fails to send your support payments on time.

Alimony, also known as spousal support or spousal maintenance, is paid by the higher-earning spouse to his former mate for her continuing maintenance, if needed, and may be paid until she dies, remarries, or becomes self-supporting. Some states provide only for "rehabilitative alimony," which is paid for a limited time to enable the former spouse to become self-sufficient, and some states do not provide for any alimony at all. Child support, on the other hand, is paid by the noncustodial parent to the custodial parent as his contribution to the support of the child. In the case of shared custody, child support is usually paid by the higher-earning spouse. Sometimes the courts award combined undifferentiated support, called family support or family maintenance, in lieu of separating support into the two categories of alimony and child support. Alimony and family support are generally taxable to the recipient, unless the payments are specifically designated as nontaxable in the marital settlement agreement. Child support is not taxable to the recipient.

If you are contemplating divorce, discuss with your attorney the possibility of putting funds aside. Amass the funds you'll need by accumulating cash reserves in your own name. If you are afraid your husband will seize your joint savings, transfer your share to a bank account in your own name. However, be aware that this act of self-protection may be perceived by your spouse as hostile and get your divorce off to a bad start. Also note that having large sums of money under your control may diminish your chances for an award of temporary alimony, and you will end up supporting yourself from marital assets rather than from your husband's current earnings.

If you haven't done so already, establish credit by applying for credit cards with check-writing privileges. Talk to your banker about obtaining an unsecured line of credit, which means credit that is not collateralized by real estate or other property.

One ready source of cash may be the equity in your home, but if you keep the house, you will end up with the responsibility for paying the mortgage, including the cash borrowed to meet financial obligations during the divorce. If refinancing the house is your only option to obtain needed funds, agree in writing with your spouse on the amount to be borrowed and for what it will be used. If there is cash left over from the refinancing, maintain control over it. Make sure that your husband doesn't claim the excess, which may leave you without funds.

If you have shared credit cards, take steps to protect your economic interests after separation. Send your creditors a letter stating that you will not be liable for any post-separation debts incurred on those accounts by your spouse, and close out as many joint accounts as possible. For any accounts that you leave open, ask each creditor to send you a statement of the account as of the date of your separation, and make sure that your creditors send you a statement every month. Although debts after separation are generally the separate obligation of the borrowing spouse, in most states post-separation purchases for the necessities of life, such as food or clothing, are the joint responsibility of both spouses until the divorce is final.

TIME YOUR ACTIONS

◇ In divorce, proper timing is very important. Don't just pack your bags, load up your children, and drive away in the second-best family car. Instead, prepare by using joint funds to undertake any necessary car repairs, for example, to pay for necessary dental work for the children, and to add proper career clothes to your wardrobe. If your husband is scheduled to receive a large bonus, and if you have access to the bonus proceeds, wait until he receives it before you leave, and put your share in your separate bank account to use while you are in the process of divorce. If you have been married for 9 years, try to stay married for 10, so that you can collect on your husband's Social Security record when you reach retirement age. Pay bills and credit cards from joint accounts before you separate, so you don't become responsible for those obligations later with no money to pay them.

Don't feel guilty or superstitious about planning for the possibility of divorce. Guilt will prevent you from taking the steps that are required if you are to have a secure future. Prepare for the possibility of divorce by gathering facts and learning everything you can about the financial aspects of your life. Understand your legal rights and financial obligations, and decide what you want, for now and the future. Because doing this will be more difficult during periods of high stress, it's wise to do it before stress sets in.

GATHER FINANCIAL RECORDS

◇ Document all the facts of the financial life you and your husband have shared. Obtain copies of loan applications, financial statements, and brokerage statements. If you can't locate them, ask bankers and brokers to supply you with copies. Secure copies of the past two to five years' joint tax returns, as well as tax returns for any partnerships or corporations that you and your husband own, and read them carefully; you may want to ask an accountant to help you interpret them if you haven't participated in their preparation. If you suspect your husband has been hiding cash, these tax returns can show where hidden assets may be buried.

Income tax returns offer excellent signposts for your financial life. For example, the interest income reported on Schedule B of one's personal tax return roughly indicates the amount of money maintained in various bank accounts. If you divide the interest reported on the tax return by your estimate of the interest rate, you will know approximately how much is in the various accounts.

For example, if your tax return shows interest income of $1,400 from Main Street Bank, and you estimate that the interest rate paid by the bank was 7 percent, divide the $1,400 of interest income by .07, and you will find that the average balance in the accounts at that bank was approximately $20,000.

If the tax return shows a deduction for a retirement plan, such as an IRA or 401(k), locate the documents that pertain to those retirement assets so they can be valued and divided. Retirement assets can be awarded to the employee spouse or divided by Qualified Domestic Relations Order (QDRO). A QDRO is served on the plan administrator and tells him to segregate the portion of the account that belongs to the nonemployee spouse and either make payments to her when the husband reaches retirement age, or pay to her now her portion of the retirement accounts. She can then make a tax-deferred rollover into her own IRA, or keep the money outside an IRA and pay tax on the funds (plus a 10 percent penalty for early distribution in the case of an IRA distribution).

If you suspect your husband has not been reporting all of his income to the IRS, combining the information on your joint tax return with an estimate of your living expenses can be unexpectedly illuminating. If the tax return shows little income and yet you and your husband live in reasonable style, unless you have been living off borrowed money, it is likely that your husband has underreported his income on the tax return.

Before you leave home, use bank statements, canceled checks, and check registers to analyze your family spending history for the past year. If you had separate property that you brought into the marriage or inherited while you were married, locate the records that prove your separate property claims. To proceed with your divorce, you must know what you own, what you owe, and what your income is. You also must know the cost of your ongoing needs and those of any dependent children. In preparing for a new future, carefully analyze the past. Such a review and analysis will help you determine your future needs and property rights, and your written summaries of the results, as well as the supporting copies of the documents, will help you control the high cost of attorney fees.

If your discussions with your husband about the divorce are acrimonious, and if he should threaten to destroy records, to ruin his business so you have no claim on its assets, to suppress income, or to hide assets, immediately write down the exact words of his threat and the time, the date, and the place it occurred. This information may be useful if you ask the judge to freeze assets, or if you allege that your husband has tried to deceive you by understating income or assets.

Systematically list all your assets, including cost and market value, so your attorney and accountant can assess the consequences of proposed property settlements. Be sure to obtain records on every asset that you want to keep or share in the divorce. If you want to keep your house, for example, you need to know not only its original cost, but the cost of all improvements made since its purchase and the amount of any prior gains that have been deferred on previous residences you have sold. If possible, try to obtain this data before you begin divorce proceedings.

IDENTIFY YOUR ASSETS

◇ When you divorce, you must identify the assets that you and your husband have accumulated and establish their value. Even if your husband has taken care of the finances during your marriage, it is now up to you to find those records. You cannot possibly arrive at an equitable settlement until you have all the financial information. You are entitled to your share of any marital property you find, and any additional income you discover may increase the amount of earnings used to compute spousal support and child support. Combining the talents of an eagle-eyed investigative (forensic) accountant with your attorney's ability to subpoena records should uncover many of these hidden assets.

You are entitled to an equitable portion of your marital assets, so be sure not to overlook any of them. Carefully inventory safe-deposit boxes, track down bank and broker accounts, and obtain copies of pay stubs, retirement plans, and insurance policies. If your spouse's business generates a good deal of cash, this is when you may want to engage a forensic CPA to search for signs of possible additional income. Don't overlook any hobbies or side businesses that may generate income, and carefully value expensive hobby equipment. Even in the case of your spouse's separate property, you may be entitled to reimbursement for your contributions of money and labor, and in some states you may be entitled to a portion of the appreciation of the property as well. If you have contributed your money or your labor to supporting your husband's education or his career, this, too, may have some value under the laws of your state.

CONSIDER TAX CONSEQUENCES

◇ Divorce can have hidden tax costs, especially during times of inflation. The major asset in many marriages is the couple's home, and it can present severe tax liabilities. For example, if your house is worth $350,000, but the $125,000 you paid for it is reduced on your tax forms by having claimed $75,000 deferred gains on prior homes you have sold, it currently will have only a $50,000 tax basis. This means that, if your combined federal and state tax bracket is 33 percent, you will be assuming a hidden tax liability of $100,000 or more if you keep the house. That tax will be payable when you sell the house, unless you buy a new one that costs at least as much as the net sales price of the old house, or unless you wait to sell it until you are 55 and can exclude $125,000 of gain under special IRS provisions. If you are planning to sell the house, you would be better off doing so while you and your husband still own it together. In that way, you will owe tax on only one-half of the proceeds, and you can escape that tax by reinvesting in a new house that costs only half of the net sales price. Note that you do not have to be married at the time of sale to effect the split of the tax consequences—owning the house together is sufficient— and if one or both of you are over 55 you will probably want to finalize the divorce before the sale so you will qualify for two $125,000 exclusions.

TAKE TIME TO EXPLORE YOUR OPTIONS

◇ Learn about your options so you can make wise decisions. Organizing the facts, searching out data, and obtaining preliminary valuations for property to be divided will open the way to exploring new possibilities. Study the legal process, investigate your finances, examine career options carefully, and see that you have become a party to all information about family financial issues. Consider what you want from the divorce, and what you need to live on. Become familiar with how the divorce process works, and how the state laws regarding child custody and support might apply to your case.

Keep in mind that this is your divorce, not your attorney's. Your attorney will give you advice, but the decisions should be up to you, regardless of how skilled the attorney is or how strong his or her opinions are. Even though it may be tempting to depend on experienced professionals at this stressful time, your staying in control of your divorce will produce the best possible conditions for a favorable settlement.

If you and your husband are able to communicate, negotiate as much of the divorce directly with him as possible, with your attorney's advice. This will often save considerable legal fees, though some attorneys advise against direct communication with your husband. If you cannot talk with each other, then let the attorneys negotiate. But in no case should you place responsibility for the details with your attorney and assume that your interests will be properly served without your active participation. When your divorce is final, your attorney will close the file and put it away. You will live with the consequences of the settlement far into the future, and it should be one that is fashioned to suit your needs.

SEPARATE MONEY FROM EMOTION

◇ Don't let your divorce turn into an emotional battleground. Although only 10 percent of divorces end up in court, many of those settled out of court are acrimonious rather than amicable, and, generally speaking, the higher the emotions, the longer the proceedings and the more costly the divorce.

Divorce is an emotional matter, to be sure, but it is also a business negotiation. Try to express your emotions at home or with friends, not in your attorney's office, where doing so will be both unproductive and expensive. Reserve your attorney's office for the business at hand.

While it may be tempting to use money as a weapon, or to be vindictive, such emotional behavior will only hamper your case.

Men usually have more trouble in coping with their emotions than women do during divorce, and your husband may manifest anger about the property issues, for example, as a way of expressing his emotions in general; battling over property and support may allow him to delay dealing with the emotional aspects of the divorce as he strategizes the economic aspects. For you, dealing with the property is probably an added burden at this time of stress, but if your husband is ready to fight over property, you must rise to the occasion so that you can be sure to emerge from the process with what is rightfully yours.

The outcome of legal action on many issues in divorce is highly predictable, so there is usually little to gain from doing legal battle. If you can keep your own emotional issues separate from the legal and financial ones that your divorce entails, you can keep your divorce under control. The more you know about the process and the earlier you take control, the more easily and inexpensively you will get through it.

BE CERTAIN TO GET YOUR FAIR SHARE

◇ In our society, most women have been socialized to be peacemakers, supportive and sensitive to the needs of others. Divorce is about survival, however, and regardless of how deeply you value human civility, you must fight for what you are entitled to, and sometimes this means fighting hard. Be sure to get what you need from the settlement, and take care not to underestimate your needs. Remember, too, that alimony is taxable, so you will need even more of it to pay the income taxes that will be due. If you have children, also provide for their future education when you negotiate a settlement.

Your husband may complain that if you claim everything you are entitled to by law, you will break him and he will be unable to survive financially. Don't be taken in by such a contention. For example, if you and your children are awarded support and end up living on 40 percent of the formerly combined income while he lives alone on the rest, he may suffer, but he will certainly survive.

While it is true that the more negotiating you can do yourself, the less expensive the divorce process will be, don't make important financial concessions to save attorney fees. If you don't stand up for your financial rights, you will regret it for the rest of your life. A husband's threat to quit his job and go on welfare may go far to convince his soon-to-be-ex-spouse that she should reduce her claims, but such threats are rarely acted on. Be firm; claiming your share is a measure of your self-regard, not an indication of the compassion of which you are capable. The following list should be of help in determining whether your husband has hidden property that should be valued and divided. Here are a few areas in which to look:

1. antiques, artwork, or hobby equipment often overlooked and undervalued, sometimes included in office furnishings
2. collusion with his employer to delay bonuses, stock options, or raises until after the divorce
3. income that has gone unreported on tax returns and financial statements (If your life-style costs have exceeded reported income, carefully document cash expenses and tradeouts with other merchants.)
4. a custodial account set up in the name of a child, using the child's Social Security number
5. a counterfeit debt repayment to a friend, with the prearrangement that the friend will hold the money until after the divorce
6. a salary paid from the spouse's business to a nonexistent employee, with the proviso that the checks will be voided after your divorce is final
7. money paid from your spouse's business to an intimate associate, such as his parent or girlfriend, for business services not rendered, earmarked for return to your spouse after the divorce is final
8. delay in signing long-term business contracts until after the divorce

9. expenses paid for a girlfriend, such as gifts, travel, jewelry, rent, or college tuition

10. evidence of investment in municipal bonds or Series EE savings bonds, for which no interest may be reported on Forms 1099 or on the applicable section of the tax return

Note that as a general rule, divorcing parties do not "hide" assets, forge fictitious loan documents, and the like. But divorce can sometimes evoke such behavior, particularly in spouses who are accustomed to underreporting taxable income to the IRS or who are emotionally unable to accept the prevailing concept that a long-term marriage is an economic partnership and the attendant asset division that accompanies the break-up of that partnership.

BE READY FOR THE WORST

◇ Don't succumb to staying in a bad marriage for purely financial reasons. If you fear not having enough money to live on after a divorce, figure out the worst that could happen to you, and then determine how you would deal with it. Who can you borrow from or move in with? Is welfare a temporary solution to restore your financial stability? After all, that is just what the welfare system was designed for: to help people who are having financial difficulties.

Many women put off acting to end a bad marriage because they don't know what they really want in the future. In divorce, that can be dangerous. Even if you are unsure of whether your marriage will be repaired or end in divorce, you needn't put off gathering vital information. Learn all you can about your financial situation, what you own, what you owe, and your family income. Gather the information first, so it will be at hand if you decide to act, or if your indecision about the marriage should be foreclosed by your spouse's actions. You may not know whether you would like to keep or sell the house, for example, but don't delay finding out how much it is worth, how the title is held, how much is due on the mortgage, and its cost basis for income tax purposes. If you are uncertain about whether to cash out your share of your husband's retirement plan or wait until he reaches retirement age to collect benefits, don't put off determining its value. If you think your marriage may be headed for divorce, find out now what is in the safe-deposit box. Once you have the information you need, you may decide never to act on it, but you won't be pressed into securing it at a moment of great stress.

Once you decide to divorce, how long will the process take? If you and your husband agree to part amicably and are willing to negotiate, it can be accomplished with relative speed. But if emotions are running high, it is best to slow down the process and give both parties a chance to gain equilibrium.

Attorneys, accountants, and other professionals who participate in the divorce process know that divorce has its own rhythm. When the divorcing couple is at odds over the settlement or over other matters, no amount of pushing will propel the divorce forward. Once the prospect of the divorce becomes a reality for each of the spouses, matters become settled quickly.

DEVELOP YOUR CAREER

◇ Perhaps you put aside your own career development in favor of your husband's career or your family. If so, divorce may force you into the workplace, even though you lack training or up-to-date credentials. In any event, divorce often provides an opportunity to get some career counseling—perhaps at a local university or community college—and to go back to school. Your settlement with your husband might provide for money for tuition, books, and living expenses while you are getting your career on track.

GET GOOD PROFESSIONAL ADVICE

◇ Once you decide to divorce, you need all the help you can afford. If you hire an inexperienced attorney, simply because he or she will represent you cheaply, you may end up with a divorce settlement that is less than you deserve.

Find a good divorce attorney by soliciting recommendations

from reputable nondivorce lawyers, recommendations from professionals who work in the divorce area, such as divorce counselors and accountants, or calling your local bar referral services. As stated previously, consult family and friends who have been through divorce recently. It's wise to interview a number of attorneys before you make up your mind. Hire one who seems to be in tune with your position, and who has the knowledge to help you get the best possible settlement for yourself.

If you and your spouse are able to communicate, consider using a mediator to help you work out some of the financial and family issues. Mediation may be useful in resolving some issues such as child custody and visitation, but may not work for other issues, such as division of marital property. Be aware that mediators seek to resolve issues by finding a middle ground, and that may not serve you well if you are under emotional stress or negotiating with an unreasonable spouse.

Engage a financial adviser to provide you with a perspective about your property settlement and its potential tax consequences. Join a support group or get individual psychological counseling to help you through the emotional crunches that you probably will experience during divorce. And take your time; this is your chance for a new beginning.

NEGOTIATING THE LEGAL ISSUES OF DIVORCE

Marriage is a legal contract, so you must take legal steps to break it. The legal part of divorce includes the disposition of property, debts, custody, and support.

Fortunately, the number of legal issues that need to be addressed in divorce is finite. After establishing what marital property there is and what it is worth, you must establish whether it is to be divided, to be held jointly, or to be sold. When appropriate, alimony must be considered, taking into account the needs of both parties, as well as the length of the marriage, the earning power of each spouse, and, if the spouse is dependent, his or her physical and emotional state. In determining child support, the ability of each parent to contribute will be taken into account, as well as what money the children already might have and their particular physical or emotional problems. Child custody and visitation schedules will also have to be worked out.

To protect your economic well-being, be aware, first, that you and your spouse now have separate, competing economic interests. He is not likely to sacrifice his own economic interests to make you happy, so be skeptical about any contention on his part that he means to do so. Second, as we have noted, you must have full knowledge of everything that you and your spouse own and owe, and you must convey this information to your attorney. Take the time to think about your financial future, formulate new goals and objectives, and communicate those to your attorney. You and your attorney, with the help of your financial adviser, can then decide what assets will serve you best in the future and what assets will serve you less adequately. To maintain a fluid negotiating process, don't take a rigid stance too early, but unless you decide in advance what assets you would like to receive in the property settlement, you'll end up with only those assets your husband does not want, and they may not suit your needs.

As mentioned, most divorces never go to trial. One of the spouses files for divorce, the parties come to an agreement, the attorneys prepare the property settlement papers, and the final agreement is submitted to a judge for signature. The rules vary from state to state, and in some states the parties may have to appear briefly before the judge.

Because a divorce never goes to trial doesn't mean that there were no disagreements. The discovery process and negotiations may be lengthy and bitter, with many depositions, notices to produce, interrogatories, appraisals, accountings, motions, and a great deal of legal maneuvering. Restraining orders may have to be imposed to keep the parties from disposing of property, or even to prevent them from doing physical harm to each other.

Remain aware that each divorce is different, and that you must adhere to your own rhythm and timetable. Strategically, it is no better or worse to take a short time or a long time in negotiating a divorce. The best way of proceeding is to decide on the big issues that you want to go your way, and then be prepared to make concessions on the issues you care less about. This will result in a better settlement and probably fewer legal fees.

Above all, remember that you should not be expected to resolve all your problems immediately. In many ways, divorce is an endurance test. You need to have the emotional stability and the physical stamina to last as long as your spouse will. Suppose, for example, that your husband is fighting to prevent you from getting your rights. His ploy may be to make you become insolvent before you can obtain an equitable distribution of your share of the property. He might assume that if he can wear you down, you'll just give up and accept whatever he offers, simply to be relieved of the pressure and conclude the process. If you are tempted to give up, don't. The rights you have in divorce are usually rights you must fight to secure, and you will have to accept the emotional and financial costs of securing them as part of the process.

With luck, you and your husband can sit down together and work out an equitable settlement. But it takes communication, understanding, and compassion to negotiate a settlement, and since those traits may be missing by the end of your marriage, it is hardly reasonable to expect that you and he can easily agree now. In any case, you will probably have to negotiate for your financial security, and negotiation will take hard work on both your parts.

In the past, if a husband wanted to end a marriage, he would have to arrange for a fair financial settlement with his wife or she could refuse to grant him a divorce. Under no-fault divorce laws, however, women have lost some of the financial leverage they once had, though in some states a "no-fault" divorce will not be granted until all economic issues are resolved. In order to secure your share of the property you and your husband own, you must act in your own best interests. Your attorney needs your full cooperation, for your husband may tenaciously oppose your claims, and if you end up in court, your attorney must be able to present the facts of your case and points of law clearly and forcefully.

Lawyers are often blamed for stirring up conflict in divorces, but the parties themselves are sometimes far more combative than their attorneys. When an attorney does create conflict, it is generally either because the client insists that the attorney demonstrate aggression, or because the attorney believes that the client is being passive and appears willing to concede more than she should. Dissension can be expensive, of course, and it sometimes appears that an attorney may be engaging in conflict simply to obtain higher fees. While some attorneys may be guilty of such behavior, clients are often unaware of the number of intricate legal issues that must be resolved to complete the case so that future misunderstandings and further legal challenges cannot ensue.

CAN YOU OBTAIN YOUR OWN DIVORCE?

◊ In most states you can obtain your own divorce, but doing so is advisable only if: your case is not complicated, your marriage was of short duration, you and your husband have no substantial assets, you have no children, and you and your husband can reach a fair and amicable settlement yourselves. If you decide to attempt to obtain your own divorce, you can secure the papers you need at your local courthouse. To help you complete the paperwork, look for a book on do-it-yourself divorce at your public library or at the local bookstore. Divorce laws change rapidly, and an out-of-date book may contain information that is no longer valid, so be sure the book you use is a current edition.

If your case is simple but the forms seem daunting, consider enlisting the help of an inexpensive legal clinic or paralegal service. But don't negotiate your divorce on your own or by way of such low-cost services if your assets are many or difficult to value, such as licenses, degrees, and professional practices. If you overlook even one marital asset to which you were entitled, or if you become responsible for one bill that your spouse should have paid, your low-priced divorce will turn out to have been very costly.

MEDIATION AND NEGOTIATION

◊ A negotiated settlement will surpass a court-ordered settlement in many ways. Because so little court time is allowed for each case, the presiding judge will have relatively little knowledge about you and your husband. As a result, there are important factors that the judge may not consider, such as the emotional value of certain property, or the latent tax consequences of the division, such as the capital gains taxes you will owe if you later sell the house, factors that you and your husband will be able to take into account as you negotiate. In addition, a protracted courtroom battle creates substantial bitterness.

On the other hand, if you and your husband are able to negotiate an agreement actively, you will both be more likely to live up to its terms, and you will probably have fewer conflicts over the years about such issues as child visitation and property rights.

Because you and your husband each have a vested interest in your divorce, the terms of settlement will be better if you can work them out together, step by step. If your husband is unwilling to negotiate with you, of course, your attorney will have to negotiate with his attorney. Once the process is launched, your husband may begin to participate in negotiations with you on a meaningful level.

You may feel unable to negotiate with your husband because you are under extreme stress, or because you are still hoping for a reconciliation. If your husband is pressing for divorce against your wishes and your own opposition to it has not abated, take your time in moving through the divorce process, but also realize the likelihood that the divorce will probably take place sooner or later. If you give your feelings of opposition time to abate, eventually you will be able to take an active role in negotiating the kind of settlement terms that suit you.

Mediation may help you resolve some of the issues in your divorce. Divorce mediation sometimes works if there are relatively few assets at stake, but if your case is complicated and your husband has more bargaining power and more negotiating experience than you do, a mediated settlement may not give you all that you are entitled to. This is because the mediator's primary job is to help you and your husband reach an agreement, and while most mediators are trained in both psychology and the law, they are usually more interested in helping you resolve your situation peaceably than in helping you secure your share of the settlement in dispute. Mediation often works well to settle the nonfinancial issues of divorce, such as child custody and visitation; in addition, disputes about the division of furniture and other such personal property usually can be settled efficiently in mediation. Look in the Yellow Pages of the phone book under "Mediation" or "Dispute Resolution" for the names of agencies in your area that specialize in mediating, or consult your local district attorney's office or county government office to locate mediators in your community.

If you decide to negotiate your own settlement, either alone or with the help of a mediator or counselor, have the settlement documents reviewed by an attorney before you sign them to make sure that you are obtaining all the assets and rights that are legally due you. You and your husband may be able to agree on some issues but not on others, and you may have to resolve the balance of the issues through attorney-assisted negotiations. If you are in doubt, engage an attorney to guide you.

Your husband may ask you not to get lawyers involved. He might say he wants to get the divorce over with quickly and tell you that he will treat you fairly. While this may be the prelude to an amicable settlement, it can also be a tactic to lull you into overlooking assets that are rightfully yours. The divorce process is such that while most husbands profess to want to conclude the divorce as soon as possible, full cooperation is rare. If your spouse genuinely wants to facilitate the divorce process and to minimize attorney fees, he will quickly provide you with all the books, records, tax returns, financial statements, and canceled checks for his business, and he will agree to answer questions under oath in deposition at your attorney's convenience. If he does not choose to cooperate, he may destroy records, hide assets, and try to persuade you that the property you want to keep has appreciated in value while the assets he wants to retain have declined considerably. He may profess that his business income has fallen substantially and even that he is on the verge of bankruptcy. He may even tell your children that you are unreasonable in your demands for a settlement. Remember that your spouse will be prudently looking after his own financial interests, and expect him to act accordingly. Even years of trust between you can become violated during a struggle over a divorce settlement.

If your husband is an expert business negotiator, or if he is in control of most of the marriage's financial assets, you will need an experienced and dedicated attorney to help you search out the assets and ensure that you get what you deserve. If your husband tells you he wants to be fair, that he is looking out for your best interests, and that he will give you the lion's share of the property, beware. Unless he is overwhelmed with guilt, you can be sure that he is looking out for his own interests, and that he will continue to do so. When he says he will give you "everything," he may mean that he will give you everything you can find, and as noted earlier, a good attorney, with the help of a qualified forensic accountant, can help you find and divide the hidden assets as well.

If you and your husband have each hired attorneys to represent you in the divorce, do not expect your attorney to negotiate directly with your husband. Your attorney may communicate only with your husband's attorney, and not with your husband himself. You are free to communicate with your husband, of course, and indeed, structured, controlled communication may help you settle your case. To keep communication on an even keel in such negotiating meetings, you may wish to include an accountant or a counselor to help you assert your rights. This third party is not an impartial mediator, but serves as your advocate, present to offer the advice and support you might need to deal directly with your husband.

CHOOSING AN ATTORNEY

◇ Choose an attorney with whom you feel comfortable, and whose advice you trust. The attorney will represent you in situations when you cannot speak for yourself, such as temporary support hearings, ex parte hearings in the judge's chambers, negotiations with your husband's attorney, and court trials. Choose an attorney who is knowledgeable and experienced, attributes that are far more important than his or her age, sex, or marital status. The following list should help you in your search:

1. Choose a lawyer who is highly experienced in divorce and divorce law.
2. Interview more than one lawyer and select one who is both sensitive and objective.
3. Choose a lawyer who is straightforward with you about

charges, retainers, and expenses; be sure you are aware of exactly what fees will be charged and when payment is expected.

4. Select a lawyer who explains the divorce process in terms you understand, without resorting to legal jargon.

5. The lawyer should answer both the questions you ask and the questions you forget to ask.

6. A responsible lawyer will be able to tell you what you can reasonably expect as settlement and support, and will not make promises that cannot be kept.

Look for an attorney who you believe really cares what happens to you, who will bolster your spirits when they flag, and who seems capable of being supportive if you become discouraged. Even if you live in a rural community and your attorney does not specialize in matrimonial law, he or she should nevertheless be well versed in the law and be willing to assert your rights to reach an equitable resolution. The attorney also should be able to give you a clear-cut idea of what to expect as he or she represents you. An attorney who is in any way compromised by a business relationship with your spouse or by any other such potential conflict of interest will be unable to act in your best interests.

To prepare for the initial interview with your attorney, gather as much data as you can about your financial situation and assets and liabilities. The attorney will need to know your basic personal and financial situation to assess the complexity of your case and to answer your questions.

Here is a list of questions to ask the attorney at your first meeting:

1. How long have you practiced law, and how long have you specialized in matrimonial law? (If matrimonial law is not the attorney's specialty, then what portion of his or her time is spent in that arena?)

2. What percentage of your cases end in a negotiated settlement rather than in a court trial?

3. Who else will be on the divorce team, such as associate attorneys and paralegals?

4.   Do you use outside professionals, such as valuation experts and accountants versed in divorce proceedings, to assist with cases?

5.   What are your hourly rates, and will I be billed extra if the outcome of my case is favorable? (It is unethical in many states to charge such additional amounts in matrimonial cases.)

6.   At what rate will I be billed for secretarial and paralegal time?

7.   How much will you charge as a retainer fee, and will the unused portion of the retainer be refunded to me if not used? (Minimum fees are regulated or prohibited in many states.)

8.   How often will I be billed, and when must I pay the balance due?

9.   Will you attempt to get my spouse to pay your legal fees?

10. How long will the case take to resolve?

11. What participation will I be able to have in the divorce proceedings, the discovery process, and the negotiations?

At the initial conference, you and the attorney need to agree on how payment will be made when the initial retainer has been used. If you lack the money to pay for the divorce and cannot borrow the necessary funds, will your attorney agree to wait until the case is concluded to collect the balance of the fees? Reach an agreement that will fit your finances, and get the agreement in writing as part of the attorney's engagement letter.

You must feel confident in your attorney's ability to represent you competently. In the adversary system, parties to legal proceedings sometimes feel more like frustrated spectators than participants, while attorneys, often delayed by other clients and proceedings, communicate with each other. You also may be reluctant to contact your attorney to inquire about possible new developments because you know you are being charged each time you call. No matter how skilled your attorney is and how well you communicate with each other, you may feel frustrated about these matters as the process winds on.

Here is what to expect from a responsible divorce attorney:

1. a clear explanation of your rights and how the attorney will work to secure those rights for you
2. copies of everything pertinent to your case, particularly correspondence with your husband's attorney
3. a detailed monthly bill showing the time that the attorney spends on your case
4. an explanation of the expenses you are expected to pay, including court costs, accountants' fees, expert witness fees, appraisal fees, etc.
5. a promise to try to negotiate a settlement rather than litigating the case, and a promise to litigate with force if necessary
6. a promise to return your telephone calls as soon as possible
7. the assurance that he or she will keep you up-to-date on settlement negotiations

Here are the initial steps your divorce attorney should take:

1. Where appropriate, petition for temporary alimony and support orders as soon as possible.
2. If you wish, make sure you have temporary possession of your car and the home.
3. Arrange for your temporary possession of the household items you want and need.
4. If there has been substantiated domestic violence, have your husband agree to leave the family home, take all of his belongings, and agree to stay away from the house.
5. Arrange for visitation for the children.
6. Make sure you and the children are covered by medical insurance.
7. When mandated by state law or warranted by your husband's actions, enjoin your husband from making changes in life insurance policies, bank accounts, stock accounts, etc.
8. Begin discovery proceedings immediately.

THE DIVORCE PROCESS

◇ To begin the divorce process, you file a petition that is served on your husband—unless he files the petition first, in which case it will be served on you. Whichever of you files the petition is the petitioner; whoever receives it is the respondent. The petition details the bare facts of the case, such as when you were married and whether there are children and assets, and also states whether you are seeking a divorce, annulment, or legal separation. In "fault" states the complaint must be specific and detailed enough to set out a cause of action for divorce. When you file for divorce, you may also want to request an injunction against your husband, enjoining him from taking and spending any of your joint assets.

If you and your husband have not reached a marital agreement, then within 30 days of receiving service of the petition, the respondent spouse must file a response. If he or she does not file a response, in some states it is assumed that the respondent agrees with all facts as stated in the petition, agrees to the petitioner's requests, and concedes on every point, in which case the divorce will go straight to a routine hearing and judgment. In other states an inquest will have to be held, which is often as complicated and time-consuming as a trial.

If you are the petitioner, and if your spouse does respond, you have a contested case. The next step is to obtain pretrial temporary orders to maintain the status quo as you move through the divorce process. Your temporary orders will govern such issues as spousal and child support, custody and visitation arrangements, asset freezes, restraining orders, and the temporary possession of such assets as the family home.

THE DISCOVERY PROCESS

◇ In the discovery process, each party attempts to discover the facts of the case. Doing so can be easy or difficult, depending how many of your financial records you already possess, and whether real estate, pensions, and businesses must be valued. In the discovery process, your attorney's job is to identify all property in which you and your husband have an interest, characterize that property with regard to whether it is marital or separate, establish the properties' value, and divide it between the two of you.

If you and your husband both know exactly what property you own and are able to agree on its character, value, and division, the discovery process will go smoothly and your divorce will be relatively inexpensive. If you do not know what property you own, and you and your husband cannot agree on its value, on whether it is separate property or marital property acquired during the marriage, and on which of you will receive it upon divorce, then the discovery process is likely to be extensive, the resulting animosity great, and your legal fees high.

To discover the extent of your property and its character and value, your attorney will send your husband's attorney a notice requesting copies of various documents. Your attorney may also send interrogatories to your husband, which are questions submitted to elicit sworn written answers from him. Your attorney may also take your husband's deposition at a meeting at which your husband verbally answers questions under oath. If appraisals and business valuations are needed, your attorney will request those as part of the discovery process. Generally, formal appraisals will not be needed if you and your husband are able to agree on the value of the property, but if there is any doubt, your attorney will advise you to obtain an appraisal.

As noted earlier, the importance of your knowing all the assets of your marriage cannot be emphasized too strongly. As you review financial records, look for loan repayments to family members and business partners. Was the money really owed to them, or is your husband using the guise of loan repayments to store cash with them until the divorce procedures have ended? If your husband owns an incorporated business, check the financial statements for loans he may have taken from the corporation. This money ordinarily would have been paid to him as salary, and it may be converted to salary again as soon as the divorce is final. Meanwhile, he will have understated his income to reduce the amount of support he must pay to you and your children.

Keep in mind that valuable business equipment may be fully

depreciated on tax returns, yet still retain considerable value. Be sure all assets are reflected at their true market value. Because depreciation is not a current expense, add it back to income when you are figuring out how much your husband earns. Personal expenses that are paid from your husband's business, such as auto expenses and entertainment, are actually additional income that should be counted when figuring child support and alimony and the value of the business.

If your husband is hiding assets, the involvement of a good accountant who knows the details and strategies of matrimonial law is important to your case. Your accountant and your attorney should work efficiently together to locate and establish financial information and devise the financial strategies crucial to your case, even if all the necessary material is not readily available.

You will probably not receive the equitable division of property promised you by the divorce laws of your state unless you are willing to fight for it. For example, your husband may contend that certain assets belong exclusively to him and, therefore, should not be subject to division—for example, his pension plan, an expensive sports car, hobby equipment, art, or furniture. At the same time, he may consider that items you assume are yours alone, such as jewelry, are a joint investment subject to valuation and division. Stand up for your rights and fight for what is yours. Don't let the stress you may be feeling about the end of your marriage keep you from taking strong steps to protect your economic interests.

When your attorney begins the discovery process, your husband may call you and complain that your attorney wants to run up large fees, and he may suggest that you both "just divide everything 50-50." If you agree and, therefore, claim half the property, half the retirement benefits, and half of his income, you may learn that he has been assuming that you will claim only your half of the property, and he believes that his retirement benefits and income belong exclusively to him.

If your husband is accustomed to being active in business matters, he may be uncomfortable waiting while his attorney negotiates with your attorney. He may attempt to pressure you into a premature settlement by asserting that the attorney fees are draining money away from you and your children, or that his business will fail unless the case is settled soon. Even if you are tempted to escape the process, don't be pressured into accepting less than you deserve simply to end the stress of the proceedings.

To ensure the support your children deserve, make certain that your husband's income is accurately stated in the legal documents he files. If you believe that he has understated his income, your attorney should focus on this issue in the discovery process, asking deposition and interrogatory questions designed to reveal hidden income. Identify your children's needs: Itemize every extraordinary expense, current and potential, such as orthodontic work, reading tutors, et cetera. And don't jeopardize your husband's prompt payments of child support each month by interfering with his visitation rights or by criticizing him to your children or to his family and friends.

As the discovery process comes to a close, negotiations will intensify as you and your husband seek to come to an agreement on as many facts and issues as possible, either through direct negotiation or negotiation through your attorneys. Some issues may be settled by mediation, some by negotiation, and some may go to trial. If you have decided in advance which issues you are adamant about and which issues you are willing to concede, matters will move relatively quickly. Remember not to concede on important issues just to make peace. You are entitled to the rights guaranteed to you by the laws of your state, and you should not be pressed into accepting anything less.

CHILD SUPPORT AND ALIMONY

◇ Today the widespread use of child support guideline schedules makes the calculation of support an accounting function that is based on the relative income and earning capacity of each parent. A judge may also take into consideration the financial needs of both parents and the children, the ages of the children, and the standard of living to which the children are accustomed.

Document every cost you have for your children. If you spent money on entertainment and vacations before the separation, your husband should share in these expenses now. The children should not be punished with a diminished life-style because their parents have decided to separate, and in some states a child's right to share in the income of a parent may not necessarily be limited to the "need" of the child. Don't settle for what is less than fair and reasonable, especially in the area of coverage for medical, dental, and psychological treatment. If your children need braces, or if your child needs psychological help, ask your husband to help provide the needed funds. Don't forget the expense of school-related activities and supplies, and anticipate the costs of a college education. Even though most states do not require your husband to pay to send your children to college, you should try to negotiate some provision for higher education in the final settlement.

When you receive child support, you are not required to account to your ex-spouse or to anyone else about how you use it. If your ex-husband contends that you are spending it frivolously, unless he is able to show that you are not providing the necessary care and maintenance to the children, he has no right to complain, no right to withhold child support, and no legal basis on which to ask the courts to order a reduction. (In most cases, the amount that the father pays for child support does not cover even half of the expenses of raising the children.) Of the 10 million mothers raising children alone, Census Bureau records show that only 40 percent were awarded any child support, and of those awarded support, only half received the full amount due them.

If you have primary custody of your children but your husband wants to claim them as exemptions on his tax return, include a clause in your agreement that you will sign the Form 8332 that gives him the right to claim the exemptions only if he has been timely in his payment of child support during the entire year.

Alimony is awarded in only 15 percent of divorces. In some states, judges consider the contributions made by one spouse to the education and training of the other when awarding alimony, but in other states, this is not taken into account. Even when alimony is awarded, most women do not collect all the payments due them. If you fear that your husband will not be reliable in making his payments and enforcement procedures will not be likely to be successful, or if your agreement terminates alimony on remarriage and you intend to remarry soon, you may be better off in agreeing on a lump-sum spousal support settlement, or accepting a relatively greater share of property at the time of the divorce in lieu of alimony. Your attorney can advise you and help negotiate a settlement that is fair to you.

Beware of trading child support for additional alimony or undifferentiated family support. Child support is nontaxable, but you will have to pay tax on alimony and family support. In addition, alimony payments generally terminate if you remarry, and courts may be more likely to reduce alimony payments than child support if your former spouse should make such applications later.

DIVORCE COURT

◇ Most divorce cases do not end up in court, and even of those that do, most could have avoided litigation. If the best settlement that your husband is willing to negotiate is far less than you would receive if you went to court, then litigation might be worthwhile, but the emotional toll can be considerable, and it can be very damaging, indeed, if you have children. If you do have children, or plan to continue common business interests, take into account that you will have to continue a relationship with your husband after the divorce is final. Consider, too, the acrimony spawned by public dissension. For many couples, prolonging a divorce battle, stretching it to court and even beyond, is simply a way of holding on to each other. If you and your husband are both aware of what you and your children can lose emotionally, now and in the future, by going to court, the knowledge may inspire each of you to be able to compromise fairly and reach a negotiated settlement.

Why do some cases go to trial and others settle? It depends on the facts and the temperaments of the parties involved. While it is clearly cheaper to negotiate and to settle without going to the expense of a trial, if one or both parties are being unreasonable about their demands, or if the facts of the case and the value of the assets are disputed, trial may become necessary. Some divorcing couples simply cannot relinquish the marriage and decide to get on with their lives without the ritual provided by a trial, and they find that only by going through the formal court action can the bonds of attachment be severed.

As in a great deal of litigation, divorce cases are often settled in the courtroom hallway just before trial. This is a very expensive road to settlement, as both parties will have spent many billable attorney hours preparing for court. If your spouse is being unreasonable and your case seems destined for trial, slow down the process in the hope of supplying a cooling-off period, after which he may settle into a frame of mind where negotiation is possible.

In some states, a pretrial settlement conference is required before you go to trial. At the settlement conference, you and your husband and your attorneys will appear before a judge who will offer you an opinion on how a trial judge is likely to rule, and he or she will try to persuade you to settle without a trial. If settlement cannot be reached, the case will go to trial in front of a judge. The trial judge then will consider the evidence presented and render a judgment, sometimes within a few weeks, but sometimes after several months or more. The judgment will then be entered and the court orders signed.

YOUR DIVORCE DECREE

◇ Your final divorce decree or judgment should dispose of all assets that are marital property, including life insurance policies and pension plan benefits. It should also dispose of all debts, by stating who is responsible for each. The divorce decree or judgment should also establish your right to any tax refunds and any liability for tax deficiencies assessed on joint returns filed by both of you.

If there is a chance that your past joint tax returns may have omitted income or overstated deductions, make sure that your settlement indemnifies you if the IRS decides to audit you or your former spouse. The IRS can seek back taxes from either of you, but with an indemnification agreement, your husband agrees that he will be responsible for any back taxes, and that he will repay you if you are forced to pay the IRS. If you doubt your husband's veracity, you probably should not file a joint tax return with him after you have separated; the IRS holds you both responsible for reporting all of the income on a joint return, and you should protect yourself from becoming responsible for paying taxes on income you know nothing about.

Your final decree will also dispose of your children through provisions for custody, both legal and physical, as well as their visitation and financial support. The specific responsibility of each of you for the children's expenses should be clearly outlined. The decree also will provide for alimony, if it is permitted by the state in your particular circumstances. The divorce decree or judgment also should state who is responsible for paying attorneys' fees and court costs, and should provide that if the agreement is breached at a later date, the party who breaches the agreement will be responsible for all legal fees and court costs required to cure such a breach. If possible, insert a clause that makes your husband liable for a late payment fee if he is delinquent in his payments of alimony or child support.

Federal tax law grants dependency exemptions for children to the custodial parent, unless that parent assigns the exemption to the noncustodial parent. If you have custody of the children and you agree to let your husband claim them as exemptions on his tax return, the divorce decree should reflect that agreement. (See chapter 7 about the conditions you should make in negotiating such an agreement and the tax consequences of doing so.) The divorce decree should also provide for the execution of all documents necessary to carry out the provisions of the agreement and separate the affairs of the parties.

When the divorce is final, be sure to obtain a court-certified copy of the decree for your files. This will be your proof that you are actually divorced, and you will need it for proof to such authorities as the Social Security Administration. Keep your marriage license on file as well; when you arrange to collect Social Security retirement benefits, you probably will be asked to prove that you were married as well as divorced.

ATTORNEY BILLS

◇ Ask your attorney to divide your bill into two parts, one that lists tax-deductible fees and another that includes the legal expenses that are not tax-deductible. For the portion that is tax-deductible, your attorney should append a certificate of counsel that states, "In the opinion of the undersigned, the amount of $X,XXX for legal services is deductible in the taxable year in which paid under the provisions of

Sec. 212 of the Internal Revenue Code as ordinary and necessary expenses incurred in connection with the production or collection of income, and in connection with determining and planning federal income taxation." Even the portion of your legal expenses that is not currently tax-deductible may become deductible when you sell assets you receive; a portion of your attorney fees can be allocated among the different assets that you receive in the settlement, and it is added to the tax basis of each.

COLLECTING SUPPORT

◇ If your ex-spouse falls more than 30 days behind in his child support payments to you, use every legal tool available to collect. Collection procedures exist that allow you to garnish your ex-spouse's wages and also to collect your outstanding child support from income tax refunds due him.

Many enforcement methods are available to your state's child support unit, which is an arm of the court. Enforcement officers first try voluntary methods of persuasion to effect compliance; if these methods fail, they turn to the basic judicial enforcement remedies, which include mandatory garnishment of wages, voluntary wage assignment, liens, garnishment of property, and attachment of assets. The Internal Revenue Service also will cooperate in collection of past-due child support, and state income tax refunds may also be subject to collection efforts. Even if your ex-husband moves away, the support enforcement office can still proceed against him under the Uniform Reciprocal Enforcement of Support Act, wherein the states agree to cooperate with each other.

If your ex-husband's income increases, in some states you may ask the courts to award additional child support. In making their determination, the courts will consider all changes in circumstances since the original award, particularly the increased needs of the child and an increased ability to pay. A change in the parents' relative financial circumstances will be considered by the court as well, so if your ex-husband's income has doubled, but your own income has doubled as well, child support may not be increased. By the same measure, if your ex-spouse demonstrates that his income has not increased while yours has, child support may be modified downward.

THE TAX NATURE OF ALIMONY AND CHILD SUPPORT

◊ If you receive alimony (sometimes called spousal support or spousal maintenance) or family support, it is included in your taxable income and tax-deductible from your husband's income if it meets all of the following criteria.

   1. *Dollars.* The payment must be made in cash, not property or services, to you or on your behalf. If your husband writes you a check for spousal support, it clearly satisfies the dollars requirement. If he writes a check to the insurance company for your auto insurance, that also satisfies the dollars requirement, since the payment was made on your behalf. But if your husband pays the mortgage on your residence, which he owns and in which you live, that payment does *not* satisfy the dollars requirement, since he is making the payment on his own behalf.

   2. *Document.* The payment must be made under a decree of divorce or separate maintenance, a written separation agreement, or another decree requiring support payments. If you and your husband are divorcing and have not signed a written agreement specifying the amount of support to be paid to you, nor has a support order been made by the courts, then any payments he makes to you will not be taxable to you nor deductible by him, as they do not satisfy the document requirement. If you are divorced or legally separated, and your husband generously pays you more than is specified in the decree or separation agreement, you will not owe tax nor will he be entitled to a deduction on the excess paid, as it was not called for in the decree or separation agreement.

   3. *Distance.* If you and your husband continue living together after divorce or legal separation, payments for spousal support won't be taxable to you nor deductible by him for income tax purposes. This provision does not apply during the "divorcing" period and before the

decree is final, so if you and your husband continue to live together for economic reasons during that period, you must pay tax on payments that he makes to you if they satisfy the other four criteria noted here. After your divorce or legal separation, he has one month from the time of the first alimony payment to move out and still satisfy the distance requirement.

4. *Death.* There can be no requirement to make payments after your death. If you are receiving alimony and your divorce decree orders that payments will continue to be made to your estate or your heirs after your death, none of the payments will be taxable to you or deductible by him. Though many agreements provide that alimony will terminate when you remarry, the income tax laws do not require such a provision for the payments to be includable in your income and deductible by your husband.

5. *Designation.* The payments cannot be designated as child support or as nondeductible payments. Child support is not taxable to you nor deductible by your husband, and this also applies to any payments you designate as nondeductible in your settlement agreement. (See chapter 7 for additional tax information about alimony and child support.)

WIDOWHOOD

PREPARING FOR WIDOWHOOD

Widowhood is a tumultuous time. Whether your husband's death is expected or sudden, you are thrust into economic self-survival at a time when you are particularly vulnerable. At a time you feel least able to cope with life, you must often make serious financial decisions that will have a lasting impact on your future well-being.

If you are lucky, you will be surrounded by loving friends and family and will have well-established relationships with legal and financial professionals who will help you through this difficult period. Even their presence, however, may not prevent you from encountering those who may attempt to control your funds or otherwise mismanage your assets.

Ninety-five percent of all women are on their own financially for a significant part of their adult lives, and the quality of your life will depend on your financial skills. It is important to know as much as you can about your financial affairs, and money management skills are imperative for you; you cannot afford to ignore your financial situation and leave it to someone else to manage. The traumatic early days of widowhood should not be spent scrambling to catch up on your financial education, and the earlier you have begun to take responsibility for your financial affairs, the better you will now be able to manage them.

Will there be enough money to continue your present standard of living if you are widowed? Will you need extensive financial advice? These important questions should be answered in advance of widowhood, and the most caring activity in which you and your husband can engage is to share your financial condition and your knowledge with each other and with your adult children, so that you will not have to become embroiled in arranging financial issues at a time when you have little emotional energy. Schedule a time now to sit down with your husband to discuss your finances frankly and openly; then update your discussion each year on a regular basis. Set a specific "contingency day" on which to do so.

If you have adult children, you may want to include them in these discussions. If you are not married, or have no adult children, plan an annual contingency day anyway, and make the same kind of reckoning. You must face the possibility of your premature death, and make sure that the future will be as comfortable and as uncomplicated as you can make it for those you leave behind. If you have children who are dependent on your care, you must provide adequately for them. If you have relatives who will have to be responsible for your estate, make their task as simple as possible. Remember, they will be mourning your death at the same time they will be dealing with your financial assets, problems, and the responsibilities that you leave behind.

PLANNING YOUR CONTINGENCY DAY

- Discuss contingency-day planning with your spouse and review Appendixes C–H together.
- Decide what information you must gather to prepare for the discussion, and designate which of you will do so.
- Set a date to meet for your discussion. Schedule three to four hours for your contingency-day planning, and decide in advance on following the discussion with some form of entertainment, like dinner and a movie.
- If your husband resists setting a date for the meeting, ask him

if he will help you gather the information you need to proceed yourself. Discuss with him what information you have and what you need, and then begin the process yourself. When you meet with him, your progress and determination may spark his enthusiasm for the project.

- If discussions about money have caused conflict in the past, ask your accountant or financial planner to be present to facilitate your financial discussions the first time. The money it costs to have your adviser present will be well spent if it results in a productive discussion.

TOPICS FOR DISCUSSION ON CONTINGENCY DAY

What are your financial assets? You must identify everything you own and what you owe before you can begin to plan for the future when one of you dies. Identify all your assets, cash, and the current income that will be available if either of you dies. (See Appendix C.) Then list all of your assets and liabilities. Be sure to examine all your insurance policies, and when you list your retirement assets consider deferred annuities and any employer death benefits, as well as retirement plans.

Are your assets sufficient? Now that you know how much you have, is it enough? How much would you need to live on? How much cash would you need immediately? Compute your immediate cash needs, the funds you will need to educate your children, your living expenses until retirement, and your retirement needs. Any shortfalls should be covered by insurance. (See Appendix D.)

If you find that you have more insurance than you think you need, you might discontinue one or more policies. Remember, having insurance isn't the same as holding lottery tickets. To collect on insurance policies you have to die.

Where are your assets invested? Discuss each asset you own so that you and your partner understand the nature of the investment, how much income it produces, what the long-range growth potential is, how safe the investment is, and the investment's marketability. (See Appendix E.)

Should any of your investments be sold? Examine each investment critically, including real estate and interests in any business. Does it fit your long-term investment objectives? What are the growth and income potentials of the investment? Too often a widow is left with investments that her husband made and controlled, and she is unsure about how he would have managed them if he were still alive. Discuss that information now. (See Appendix F.) Carefully consider the criteria that will indicate the time to sell investments you may now own, so that you can decide whether to continue to hold the investments as you review your portfolio each year.

Will you be able to manage this investment on your own? An active business or real estate investment requires time and skill to manage. If your husband has managed the business or property in question, and you decide that you will have the time to manage it if you survive your husband, or if selling the investment might take a long time, you must identify and develop the necessary management skills. (See Appendix G.)

Whose advice should you solicit? Which key advisers know the most about your financial and legal affairs? Both you and your husband should meet with your advisers, and each of you should feel comfortable with them. (See Appendix H.)

UPDATING ALL FINANCIAL RECORDS

◇ You shouldn't have to locate missing assets or research complex financial records in times of emotional stress. Gather financial data and update records now, including documents that detail ownership, how title is held, Social Security records, credit reports, etc.

Here are the steps to take to update your financial records:

1. Gather important papers, including financial statements, tax returns, loan documents, deeds, stock certificates, military

records, birth certificates, marriage certificates, and divorce papers from prior marriages. Place these papers in one safe location that is known to both of you.

2. On a separate page or pages, make a list of each investment, debt, and retirement plan, and indicate how title is held, what document or other material provides evidence of the investment, where it is stored, and who is its administrator or other agent.

3. Obtain a copy of the Social Security record for each spouse by calling 1-800-234-5772 and asking for Form 7004, "Request for Earnings and Benefits Estimate Statement." Once it arrives, review it for completeness.

4. Request and then review a copy of your credit report from TRW, Equifax, or TransUnion, the three major national credit bureaus. (You can find them in your Yellow Pages under "Credit Reporting Agencies.") Report any inaccuracies to the credit-reporting institution, and request that corrections be made in the report. Send a copy of your letter to the creditor that provided the incorrect information.

5. If the credit bureau has failed to correct the information in your file, place a statement of 100 words or less in your credit file at the relevant credit-reporting institution, explaining any inaccurate or misleading information contained in your credit file. Note in your covering letter your understanding that the institution is required to include it in all replies to requests for your credit rating.

6. For each current credit card, note whether each spouse is a primary cardholder or merely an authorized user. Then make sure that both spouses have credit cards in their own names for which each is individually liable, as opposed to being designated as only a secondary user whose credit is based on the earning power of the other spouse.

REVISING OR UPDATING YOUR WILLS

◇ You and your spouse will ensure that your estate passes to others in accordance with your wishes by being certain that your wills say what you want them to say. Will the assets be tied up in a confusing cobweb of trusts? If either of you does not have a living will, which specifies the circumstances under which you might not want to be kept alive, this is the time to make one.

Here are the steps to take to revise or update your wills:

1. Establish or review the wills of both spouses and make sure that they reflect the current intentions of each:
   a. Does each spouse understand and accept the provisions of any testamentary trusts?
   b. Have the financial needs of any of the beneficiaries changed since the will was written?
   c. Has each spouse considered establishing an inter vivos revocable trust, or "living trust," in order to avoid probate? (See chapter 8.)

2. If such a living trust exists, review its provisions. Are all assets titled in the name of the trust?

3. Does each spouse have a living will? If not, discuss the kinds of judgments each spouse expects of the other in the event his or her condition is terminal, and obtain a model document to be used in specifying these matters. Write: Concern for Dying, 250 West 57 Street, New York, New York 10017.

4. Has each spouse executed a durable power of attorney?

5. Has each spouse indicated organ-donor information on driver's licenses? Contact your department of motor vehicles for the form needed to specify organ donor information.

6. Has a letter of instruction been prepared listing the items to be given to particular individuals? There is no set format for such a letter, so you can use the style most comfortable for you, so long as the letter is dated and clearly labeled as a letter of instruction regarding the disposition of your personal possessions. The letter can be a simple listing of the items you own and whom you wish to have them, or it can elaborately describe the history of each item and explain your reasons for wanting a particular individual to inherit it. Your will should state that you intend to leave a letter of instruction regarding disposition of certain items that belong to you.

DESIGNING A PERSONAL
FINANCIAL EDUCATION PROGRAM FOR THE YEAR

◇ Extend your financial education now through reading and attending financial-planning seminars or courses. A regular program of financial education will help you prepare for the day you may be solely responsible for your own or your family's finances. (Appendix J.)

SOCIAL SECURITY SURVIVOR'S BENEFITS

◇ If your husband is covered under the Social Security system, he will receive his benefits on retirement, and you are also entitled to benefits, based on your own Social Security earnings record or spousal benefits equal to 50 percent of his benefit amount, whichever is greater. After his death, you will receive widow's benefits equal to his benefits (or your own earned benefits, if greater). If you have children under 18, they will each receive 75 percent of your deceased husband's benefits, and you may also be eligible for a 75 percent Mother's Benefit if you are not yet of retirement age, all subject to a maximum family benefit ceiling.

To obtain an estimate of future Social Security benefits you and your husband will receive, ask your local Social Security office for Form 7004. After they receive the completed form, the Social Security Administration will mail you a statement of total wages and self-employment income credited to your record and an estimate of future Social Security retirement benefits and current disability and survivor benefits.

WHEN THE DEATH
OF YOUR SPOUSE SEEMS IMMINENT

◇ Many people say "If I die" rather than "When I die." Facing the inevitability of death is difficult, but all of us owe it to our survivors to do so. You and your partner should discuss funeral arrangements and agree on them so the survivor will feel clear about the agreement during that difficult time. Be as specific as possible about funeral arrangements, including burial or cremation. (See Appendix I.)

As death approaches, planning can no longer be put off. One widow said sadly, "I knew my husband was dying, but I succumbed to magical thinking: I thought that if we didn't plan for his death, I was somehow bargaining for him to stay alive. He died anyway, of course, and I have often wished we had made plans for his death together."

When death seems near, here are some special steps to take in addition to contingency-day planning:

- Locate and review wills, trusts, and other important papers.
- Execute a durable power of attorney to take effect upon your spouse's incapacitation.
- Review beneficiary designations on life insurance and retirement programs, including VA life insurance, IRAs, and other life insurance policies. Do not designate your estate as beneficiary, as that will subject the insurance proceeds to the costly and time-consuming process of probate and administration costs.
- Consider a living will, as well as organ and tissue donations.
- Transfer additional assets to living trusts, life insurance trusts, or joint ownership, and make gifts, where appropriate, to avoid probate—which can sometimes freeze assets for years—and reduce estate taxes.
- Transfer vehicle titles to survivors, a transaction accomplished far more easily before death occurs.
- Remove important records such as wills, deeds, and trust documents from safe-deposit boxes, and place the records in a safe place at home. After death, the boxes may be legally sealed, and you may need access to the records to begin estate administration.
- Sell stocks and bonds that have decreased in value since you bought them, thus realizing the loss for offset against other income on your tax return. If you do not sell now, the tax basis in those stocks and bonds will be adjusted downward to their value at the date of death, and therefore those losses will not be realized upon a sale after death.

- Apply for credit cards in your own name, if you do not presently own such credit cards.
- Identify sources of cash to fund immediate cash needs, and make sure you will have access to adequate funds.
- Discuss funeral or memorial service arrangements, and contact clergy or other service conductors.
- Notify close friends and relatives.

WHEN YOUR SPOUSE DIES

In the United States, 1 out of every 6 women over the age of 40 is a widow, nearly 12 million widows in all. Whether your husband's death is sudden and unexpected, or whether he dies after a long debilitating illness, the impact of widowhood is powerful. You must cope with numerous details under great emotional stress.

During the first few days after your husband's death, try to make sure that someone is in your home at all times. Unfortunately, your home is a prime target for any thief who knows of your bereavement. If you are not presently widowed, but your husband is very ill, it is also important to have your house occupied or otherwise secured while you are at your husband's bedside during hospital stays.

When your husband dies, there are many urgent details to be looked after. Immediately notify the family and close friends who will come to your aid and whom you would like to have around you during the next few days. Ask them to notify more extended family, friends, and business colleagues who should be told the news in the first days following your husband's death.

FUNERAL ARRANGEMENTS

◇ If your husband died in a hospital or nursing home, the hospital will call a mortuary to arrange for the removal of your husband's body. If he died at home, you and your family may have to take care of arranging for this.

When you visit the mortuary to make funeral arrangements, take someone with you who is calm and able to help you make practical decisions about costs and services. If you and your husband talked about funeral arrangements ahead of time, take with you the notes you made, and let your friend review the notes to make sure your husband's wishes are followed. Tell the funeral director what you want, and don't be influenced by guilt, subtle social pressures, or other emotional tactics that may be employed to persuade you to spend more than you intended on a casket, a cremation urn, or other services. Most funeral directors are sincere and honest, but they are also salespeople who have little knowledge of your financial circumstances, and since their objective is to make a profit, they might encourage you to spend far more than you had planned or can afford. If your husband was eligible for Veterans Administration burial benefits, you will be asked to assign them to the funeral director as partial payment. You will have to discuss the payment of the balance of the cost of the funeral at the time you make the arrangements. Get a written agreement that includes all expected charges.

When you meet with the funeral director, tell him or her that you require at least 10 copies of the death certificate. You will need to send a copy to each insurance company from which you intend to collect, and you will need a copy when you apply for Social Security and U.S. veterans' benefits. Death certificates will also be needed for probate filings, federal and state estate tax returns, and final income tax returns.

DEATH NOTICES

◇ In many cities and towns, obituaries are published in the local newspaper. It may give you and your family comfort to write the obituary yourselves. If you choose not to do so, the funeral home will usually provide information to the obituary column of your local newspaper, including the date and place of funeral arrangements. In addition, you may wish to compose an announcement to send to your acquaintances that tells of your husband's death, when and how he died, what services were held, and where memorial contributions may be made and condolences sent. Ask one of your close friends or family members to compose the announcement for your review, unless you want to prepare it yourself.

BEGINNING THE LEGAL PROCESS

◇ Let your attorney know immediately of your husband's death so that he or she can start probate proceedings, including the notification of death and filing the will. The attorney who drew up your husband's will can guide his estate through probate, if you feel comfortable with the attorney and his or her paralegal with whom you will probably be working. If you have decided not to continue using this attorney, and have not made other plans in advance, ask friends and other attorneys to recommend a good probate attorney. Then make an appointment to interview that attorney. Find out his or her background and qualifications, and ask for an estimate of the costs that will be involved in settling your husband's estate.

As you proceed through the first months of widowhood, you may find that you lack concentration, memory, and even objectivity. This is normal, so don't be alarmed, but do be prepared. Carry a notebook with you at all times, and write down everything that may be of importance later.

Because the early days of widowhood are a period in which things easily get misplaced, put all bills into a file marked "Unpaid Bills" as they arrive and leave them in a visible place until you pay them. Create additional files for death-related papers, such as those pertaining to probate, insurance claims, income taxes, estate taxes, attorneys, accountants, appraisals, and trusts.

When you have an important meeting with an attorney, trust officer, insurance agent, or accountant, try to take a close friend or family member with you. It will not be an imposition, since friends and family are usually eager to be of help to you in specific ways at this time, and their presence will be a comfort and steadying influence. The friend can take important notes during the meeting and help provide you with clear, logical reasoning.

Be sure not to sign anything you don't fully understand. If a document is unclear to you, ask that it be explained in terms you do understand. Don't be intimidated, even if others show impatience. Proceed at your own pace, even if you think others believe that you should be moving faster. The following checklist can serve as a reminder of steps to be taken immediately after your husband's death and during the weeks that follow:

THE FUNERAL HOME
- Consider bequeathal of the body or donation of body parts and organs.
- Select an undertaker to remove the body from the place of death.
- If the body will be transported out of town, contact undertaker in locality where service will be conducted.
- Decide on type of disposition.
- Decide on the type of service to be conducted.
- Discuss costs with the undertaker. Be sure you have decided in advance on the price range you can afford, and don't waver from this decision.
- Decide on the inclusion or omission of flowers, and what to do with the flowers after the funeral (many hospitals and nursing homes will accept them).
- Notify pallbearers you have chosen.
- Order at least 10 copies of the death certificate.

NOTIFICATION OF DEATH
- Notify close friends and relatives. You may want to send a death announcement to others.
- Notify your husband's employer or immediate supervisor.
- Prepare an obituary to be sent to the local newspapers and paid notices, if applicable. Include age, cause of death, place of birth, colleges attended, degrees received, occupation and major organizations where employed, honors received, military service, if any, membership in professional organizations, immediate survivors, and time and place of services.
- Prepare announcement to be sent to friends, business associates, distant relatives, and the like, and arrange for print-

ing. Make list of people to whom announcement is to be sent.

- Set up system for acknowledgment of cards, letters, and phone calls received, and designate those who will accept phone inquiries and messages.
- Notify your banker.
- Notify fraternal organizations, and ask about what death benefits they provide, if any.
- Notify credit card companies. Some may cancel the debt.
- Notify lessors.
- Notify life insurance companies.
- Notify other insurance carriers (homeowners, auto, etc.).

HOUSEHOLD ARRANGEMENTS

- Arrange for someone to stay at the house when you cannot be there, such as during funeral services.
- Arrange for family and close friends to help with housekeeping and food preparation chores during periods that visitors are being received.
- Arrange for care of any young children in the family during the days immediately following death.
- If out-of-town family or friends are expected, make arrangements for their lodging.

PROBATE AND ADMINISTRATION

- Contact the attorney who will handle the probate.
- Locate your husband's will and review the provisions of both the will and any trusts.
- Petition the court for the appointment of an executor or administrator.
- File the will with probate court, and open the probate process.
- Apply for an estate federal identification number from the IRS.
- Open a bank account for your husband's estate.
- Apply to the probate court for a family allowance.
- Request safe-deposit box clearance from state taxing

authorities, if contents were not removed before box was sealed.

- Inventory all assets and liabilities.

INSURANCE

- Review credit card agreements to see if they may have supplied free life insurance coverage on your husband.
- Request a policy search questionnaire from The American Council of Life Insurance, Policy Search Department, 1001 Pennsylvania Avenue, N.W., Washington, D.C. 20004, enclosing a stamped, self-addressed envelope.

DEBTS

- Determine whether you have credit life insurance coverage and, if in effect, discontinue paying those covered debts.
- List all unpaid bills (use the categories "Estate, Joint, and Survivor" or "Him, Us, and Me").
- Don't pay bills that are not your legal obligation.

BENEFITS

- Notify all retirement plan administrators of your husband's death.
- If your husband was a veteran, call the Veterans Administration to get VA Pamphlet 27-82-2, "A Summary of Veterans Administration Benefits."
- File for any civil service death benefits that may be payable.
- Visit your local Social Security office to file for benefits. Be sure to bring a certified copy of your husband's death certificate.
- Contact unions, credit unions, and fraternal organizations to which your husband belonged to find out about any death benefits.
- Inquire about employer death benefits, sick leave, vacation pay, and worker's compensation benefits.

SEARCH FOR MISSING ASSETS

- Make a thorough search for possible miscellaneous death benefits payable through credit card companies, credit life insurance policies, auto clubs, auto insurance policies, and accidental death policies.

- Sort through files and desks to locate all important papers.

FINANCIAL

- Make arrangements to continue your husband's business on an emergency basis.
- Review buy/sell agreements for your husband's business, if any.
- Estimate your financial needs for the year and identify sources of cash. If there is a shortfall, decide how you are going to meet it. (See chapter 8.)
- Estimate estate taxes and administrative costs. (See chapter 8.)
- Review your investment portfolio for the possibility of any immediate changes needed.

PROBATE

◇ If your husband's estate did not contain much money or many assets, and his will leaves everything to you as surviving spouse, the laws of your state may allow you to settle the estate without becoming involved in bureaucratic administrative procedures. In that case, you will need only minimal legal help, which you might obtain through your family attorney or from the legal aid service in your community.

If your husband died intestate—without a will—the probate court will appoint a representative to handle the settlement of his estate, and your family's inheritance rights will be determined in accordance with the laws of your state.

The purpose of probate is to authenticate your husband's will, to appoint an executor or administrator of the estate, to satisfy creditors, to provide for collection of taxes due the federal and state governments, to distribute assets to the proper heirs, and to protect the rights of surviving minors and incompetents. In the probate process, the rights of inheritance will be established in accordance with your husband's will or with the laws of your state if there was no will. You or the administrator of your husband's estate will file with the probate court a list of everything your husband owned at his death. You will advertise the commencement of probate in your local newspaper, and all claims by creditors against the estate must be made during a set period thereafter. The proven debts of your husband's estate will then be paid from the assets of the estate.

If you or members of your family wish to handle certain aspects of the probate and estate settlement, reach an agreement with the attorney about which tasks you will assume and which will be left to the attorney and paralegal. Make a list of the tasks you agree to take on, and have the attorney sign the list. That way, if the attorney should later bill you for having performed the tasks, you will be better able to persuade him or her to delete these particular charges from the billing.

Not all assets your husband owned will have to go through the probate process. Any assets that he held in joint tenancy with you or another person will bypass probate and be transferred directly to you or the other joint tenant. Similarly, any assets held in the name of a living (inter vivos) trust will bypass probate and be distributed in accordance with the terms of the trust document. In some states, probate is not required if all of the assets pass to the surviving spouse. Assets that are written in beneficiary form will also bypass probate and go directly to the beneficiaries. Life insurance falls into this category, unless the named beneficiary is the estate. Other assets written in beneficiary form include annuities, IRAs, Keogh plans, and U.S. savings bonds.

TESTAMENTARY TRUSTS

◇ Many husbands leave assets to their wives in a series of complex trusts, administered by the trust department of a bank or an individual trustee. Such trusts are generally established to take advantage of professional management and administration provided by the corporate or individual trustee, and to save estate taxes through the structure of the trusts.

The most common trust structure is the standard "A-B Trust." The will provides that the property will go into two trusts upon the testator's death (testamentary trusts), the A Trust and the B Trust. For estates over $600,000, two trusts will save the maximum amount of estate taxes, because a person can leave an unlimited amount of assets to his spouse, and up to $600,000 collectively to other heirs, without paying estate taxes. If one spouse leaves the entire amount to the other spouse, when the inheriting spouse dies, her entire estate over $600,000 will be subjected to onerous taxes.

If the husband seeks to avoid such a situation by leaving $600,000 tax-free to other heirs and the balance of his estate to his wife, his wife may not have enough to live on. Consequently, the ideal estate-planning tool is the A-B Trust arrangement, whereby $600,000 is left to other heirs in a bypass trust (the B Trust), specifying that all of the income from this trust should go to the wife during her lifetime. The balance of the estate is left in a marital deduction trust (the A Trust), from which the wife will receive all of the income and as much of the principal as she needs or wants. The wife usually has access to the assets in the bypass B Trust for health, education, support, or maintenance. By limiting access, her husband has ensured that this trust will not be taxable in her estate upon her death, and that it will pass free of tax to the heirs named in the trust.

While this complex arrangement is primarily a tax-saving device, unfortunately it adds complexity to your life as a widow. You may find yourself dealing on a regular basis with a trustee with whom you have limited rapport. Here are some suggestions for establishing a productive relationship with the trustee:

- Remember that in establishing the trust your husband was not trying to control your spending, but intended, instead, to control taxes and to thus leave you a greater amount of money on which to live.
- The trustee is on your side—or should be. Although he or she has certain fiduciary obligations under the trust agreement, it is not the trustee's money, and he or she has no reason to want to displease you, the beneficiary.
- Get to know the trustee as a person, if possible. Invite him or her to lunch, and make sure that you are explicit about your needs and concerns.
- Decide with the trustee when and how you will receive pay-

ments, and in what amounts they will be. If you find that you need more money, construct a budget and discuss it with the trustee.

- Ask the trustee, an attorney, or your financial adviser to explain the various phrases in the trust agreement. If the agreement states that the trust principal is available for your health, education, support, or maintenance, make sure that whatever request you make for additional funds clearly falls into one of those categories, and that you delineate it as such.

If you use trusts in your own estate planning, make certain that you are familiar with their provisions, and that your heirs understand the reasons you have constructed the trusts so they do not question or resent the trust arrangement after your death.

CLAIMS FOR AND AGAINST THE ESTATE

◇ The probate of your husband's estate may be complicated by a number of other legal matters. His will may be contested by disgruntled heirs, such as children from a previous marriage. You or your husband's estate may file a wrongful death action against parties you believe were responsible for his death. You may have to file collection actions to recover debts that were owed to your husband or to his business before his death. You may have to defend yourself against lawsuits in which your husband was named as a defendant. Or your joint obligations with your husband, complicated by the expenses of his last illness and probate, may overwhelm your resources. If the latter occurs, you may need to file for protection from creditors under federal or state bankruptcy laws.

LIVING EXPENSES AND DEBTS

◇ The probate process takes time. In most states, for example, creditors have four months to file their written claims against the estate with the probate court. To establish the value of your husband's estate, some of the property he owned may need to be professionally appraised, and appraisals take time. While the estate is being probated, obtaining money to pay your living expenses can become a problem. Bank accounts you and your husband held as joint tenants with right of survivorship will pass to you immediately upon your husband's death. Life insurance benefits will be a source of cash for you. It will take two to six weeks after you file your claim for you to collect these proceeds. If the cumbersome probate process leaves you without enough money for your living expenses, most states have provisions for you to receive a family allowance from the estate to help you meet your financial obligations during the probate period.

Credit cards may help you through the months when cash is not readily available to pay for necessary living expenses (although usually at a high rate of interest). By law, your credit cards cannot be revoked simply because your marital status has changed, but if your credit was based on your husband's earning power, and the credit was in his name, you may need to reapply for credit cards and charge accounts. As a practical matter, you may wish to delay for a time notifying credit card companies of your husband's death, and thus evade the red tape involved in changing credit and escape the possibility that you might be turned down for credit or have the available credit limits reduced.

With certain exceptions, you are not obligated to pay debts that your husband incurred. The exceptions include debts that were secured with property, and those for which claims are filed against the estate itself. The only assets that should be used to pay these debts are the assets of the estate. You are not obligated to pay a creditor who has not filed a claim against the estate, and you are not obligated to use your separate property to pay any claim against the estate. If you have any doubts about which debts should be paid and which should not, make a list of the unpaid bills and their sources and ask your attorney to review it before you write the checks.

As mentioned previously, any assets that were held by the two of you as joint tenants while your husband was alive will pass to you upon his death without having to go through the probate courts. Title to these assets will be transferred to you automatically, upon your showing proof of your husband's death. Similarly, proceeds from life insurance policies on which you were named as beneficiary belong to you, not the estate. These assets are protected from claims against the estate, unless the debt was a joint obligation. If you are jointly obligated on a debt, and there are not enough estate assets to pay the debt, you may be required to pay the debt from bank accounts and life insurance proceeds that are not a part of the probate estate. In addition, if some debts are secured by estate property that you do not wish to be sold, you may wish to reaffirm these debts as your own and make arrangments to pay them from other nonprobate property.

With these few exceptions, you are not obligated to pay any other debts incurred by your husband, even if his unsecured debts exceed the probate estate. If that is the case, those debts will go unpaid. For example, if your husband died after a lengthy illness, he may have incurred a large number of outstanding hospital and doctor bills that are not covered by medical insurance. Unless those bills are a joint obligation under the laws of your state, it is not your obligation to pay them, and you should not do so, even if such creditors as hospitals, physicians, and other medical personnel, or bank card companies demand payment from you. Ask your attorney for specific advice about how to handle these calls.

SEARCHING FOR ASSETS

◊ If you have regularly met in advance with your spouse to discuss your financial situation, you will have most of the documents you need now readily accessible. If you have not, you will be gathering them now.

As you sort through desks and drawers, collect all papers that relate to assets owned by you and your husband. In particular, look for insurance policies, investment records, and retirement plans. Locate all bank, credit union, and savings accounts. Find the keys to all safe-deposit boxes. Keep an eye out for documents that may list any miscellaneous death benefits, such as credit life insurance designed to pay back a loan if the borrower dies, accident policies, burial policies, disability benefits, employee stock-ownership plans, and pension plans from former employers. Many credit card companies now offer free

$1,000 death benefit policies. Contact each credit card company in writing or by telephone to see if such a policy exists for your husband.

Contact your mortgage company, auto loan finance company, and any other company to which your husband owed money, and determine whether any credit life insurance policy is in place to pay off the debt at the time of your husband's death. If such a policy exists on your mortgage, you will not need to make any more mortgage payments after your husband's death. The same may be true of auto loans and other debts.

The proceeds from credit life insurance will be paid directly to the creditor. Credit life insurance is usually a decreasing term policy—the amount of the life insurance decreases as the amount you owe on the loan is reduced. Excess proceeds from the credit life policy, if there are any, would be paid to the estate.

If you are named as beneficiary of a policy, the proceeds will be paid directly to you. Even if the policy was purchased for the purpose of paying off the mortgage if your spouse died, you may not wish to do so. If your mortgage interest rate is particularly favorable, you might want to collect the life proceeds if you can invest them for a higher return than your mortgage interest rate. For example, if the interest rate on your mortgage is 6 percent, but you can invest the life insurance proceeds in bonds or certificates of deposit earning 8 percent, you would be better off collecting the life proceeds, buying certificates of deposit, and continuing to make monthly payments on your mortgage as they come due. Of course, the security of not having to make any more mortgage payments may outweigh the benefit of having the money paid to you directly and then investing it at a nominally higher rate. Consult a financial adviser to discuss what would be most appropriate in your case.

LIFE INSURANCE PROCEEDS

◊ Contact your husband's life insurance agent as soon as possible after his death. Ask him to prepare the necessary life insurance claims for you to sign, so that he can file them with the insurance company as soon as possible. If you do not have a local agent, write directly to the life insurance company to let them know your husband has died. They will send you the documents required to make a claim on your husband's policy. If you and your husband have used other insurance companies in the past, write to them and ask them to search their files for any policies currently in force on your husband's life.

Your husband's insurance policies may provide you with several options for payment upon his death. In some cases, you and he may have chosen the payment option when the policy was first purchased. If so, that choice is probably now irrevocable and cannot be changed. In other cases, however, it may be up to you to choose the payment option that suits you best. Available options vary from policy to policy, but usually they include several of the following:

- *Lump-sum settlement.* This is by far the most common option. If you choose a lump-sum settlement, you will be paid the entire face value of the policy, plus interest, if applicable, within a few weeks of filing your proof of claim.
- *Fixed-period option.* If you choose this option, you will be paid a specified amount over a fixed number of years. Each payment you receive will be partially principal and partially interest. The principal will come to you tax-free, but you will have to pay income tax on the interest each year.
- *Fixed-amount option.* The payment will be of a specified amount, and will be made to you until the insurance fund is exhausted. Each payment will include both principal and interest.
- *Life-income option.* You will receive payments of a specified amount for the rest of your life. The amount you receive each month will depend upon your age at the time payments begin. Each payment will include interest on which you must pay income taxes.

Generally, the rate of interest paid by insurance companies under the various payout options is not as great as the rate you could receive by taking the lump-sum settlement and investing the money yourself, and the opportunity for diversification of your investment among different investment categories is lost if you leave the money on deposit with the insurance company. In addition, funds left on deposit are vulnerable to loss if the insurance company becomes insolvent.

Taking Charge of Your Finances

◇ When you are able, visit the Social Security Administration. Take with you your Social Security number, your husband's Social Security number, a copy of the death certificate, your marriage certificate, and the birth certificates of any children under the age of 18. You will be eligible for immediate benefits if you have children under the age of 16, if you are 60 or older, or if you are at least 55 and are disabled. Your children may also be eligible for benefits if they are under 18. Even if you are not currently eligible for Social Security payments, fill out a Form 7004, "Request for Earnings and Benefits Estimate Statement," so that you can review records of your husband's work history to make sure that no records of wages have been excluded.

If you have children in college, ask them to visit the financial aid office at their university to see if they are eligible for increased financial aid as a result of the death of their father. Since requirements differ from state to state and college to college, it would be best if your children visited the office in person to find out. You can write or call the financial aid office, if you prefer not to burden your children with this task.

The Financial Recovery Process

◇ Certain timetables cannot be ignored. The tax return for your husband's estate is due nine months after the date of his death. Annual income tax returns for the estate will be due each April 15 or later with extensions until the estate is closed and its assets are distributed to his heirs. Other than these strict timetables, the rest of the financial recovery process is yours to accomplish at your own pace.

If you have not already done so, soon you must begin to sort through your husband's belongings, either alone or with the help of a relative or friend. If you give his clothing and personal items to a charity, ask for a receipt to use for claiming an income tax deduction for your donation.

Once you have solved immediate problems, it is time to deal with money, or lack of it. If you are struggling to make ends meet and that condition will continue, you must learn to manage the money you do have wisely. If you have received a lump-sum insurance settlement, be very careful about how you invest it. You must manage it well to continue a reasonable standard of living.

Even if you are financially comfortable, you may find your new financial responsibilities overwhelming as you assume the tasks of supervising investments, managing businesses, and generally conducting your personal financial life alone. While you may have inherited enough assets to command the personal attention of top professionals, large financial firms may assign you to the care of legal assistants, associate accountants, and bank tellers rather than assigning your business to attorneys, CPAs, and bank officers. Use the power of your money to obtain personal assistance and service from senior professionals, and assert your claims to the kind of professional attention you are due.

Take control of your financial life as soon as you are able. Many widows without experience in financial management have become victimized by incompetent or calculated mismanagement, even years after their husbands' deaths. Be suspicious if you are pressured to make investments in risky limited partnerships and other such instruments that yield high commissions for the broker or other salesperson, and conversely, be wary of low-yield investments that expose your money to the ravages of inflation. Beware of financial advisers who seem to put their own interests before yours, or who are eager to assure you about the safety of investments they cannot possibly guarantee.

If your husband complained bitterly about taxes, you might assume that taxes will be your major financial concern as well, but this is probably not true. Without your husband's earnings, you are probably in a lower tax bracket than you were before his death.

You can begin now to take charge of your finances, but it will take time before you will be focused enough to make well-considered long-term decisions. Don't move out of your home in the first year of widowhood unless you cannot afford to stay there, or unless you are entirely sure that it is the best practical move for you. (See chapter 7.)

If you can live off the interest your money earns, plus your own earnings, then spend as little principal as you can during the first year of widowhood. This will give you time to become aware of your financial needs, note and guide your spending habits, and assess your future needs for funds. Use the following checklist to help you take charge of the financial aspects of widowhood:

PROBATE AND ADMINISTRATION
- Have property appraised.
- File any wrongful death claims if your husband died in an accident or other unusual circumstances.
- Meet with the trustee of any trusts to determine procedures.
- Defend against hostile claims on the estate.
- Prepare IRS Form 706 and applicable state tax forms.
- Prepare IRS Form 1041 for the estate.
- Change the title for any joint tenancy assets.
- Change the titles to vehicles.
- Change the titles to real estate and other such property.
- Collect amounts owed to the estate.
- Prepare an accounting of estate receipts and disbursements for the courts.
- Disburse assets in accordance with the will, or with the laws of intestacy.

INSURANCE
- Decide on pertinent life insurance payout options.
- Change homeowners and auto policies to reflect new ownership.

DEBTS
- Review the claims of creditors on your husband's estate.
- Pay all funeral and administrative expenses.
- Carefully observing the exceptions allowed, pay all other debts of the estate after advertising and assessing its liquidity.
- Cancel relevant book club memberships, health club memberships, and magazine subscriptions.

BENEFITS
- Find out from the American Legion or VA the veteran's benefits to which you may be entitled (educational assistance, employment preference, GI loans).
- Ask college-age children to visit the financial aid office of their university to see if they are eligible for increased financial aid.
- File health insurance claims.
- Claim the $5,000 death benefit exclusion on your income tax return.

SEARCH FOR MISSING ASSETS
- Call your state controller's office to inquire about unclaimed property in your husband's name.

FINANCIAL
- Make arrangements for continuing your husband's business or selling it.
- File income tax returns for the estate and for any trusts.
- Avoid making major financial or life-changing decisions, such as selling your home.
- Spend as little principal as possible.
- Review your financial situation and establish new financial goals.
- Compile your financial needs, control your spending habits, and assess your future need for funds.
- Restructure your investments accordingly.

Find a financial adviser you trust and take responsibility for your own investing by drawing on his or her expertise, but maintaining control in deciding about the nature of your portfolio and its contents. (See chapter 4.)

7

ON YOUR OWN AGAIN

THE CAREER CHALLENGE

Most people want and need a challenging career, and this is often particularly true of women after divorce or widowhood. Work plays an important role in life, producing not only self-esteem and intellectual enjoyment, but valuable social relationships that often carry over to our personal lives. If your work is satisfying, you will look forward to performing it every day.

Finding a satisfying career is an enormous job in itself, and one that you might repeat several times during your lifetime. According to statistics, people change careers about three times during their lives. Especially if you have been divorced or widowed, chances are that you are now at such a crossroad. You may be ready to change careers, you may want to improve the career you already have, or you may be entering the job market for the first time in years.

THE CAREER SEARCH

◇ If you are about to begin working for the first time, if you have been a full-time wife and mother and you are now returning to work, or if your present job seems dull, unfulfilling, or dead-ended, you must assess your aptitudes and abilities, your salary requirements, and your opportunities for advancement and social interaction and begin to define the job you want.

While you need a career that uses your abilities and reflects your aspirations, your choice may have to satisfy a variety of other conditions as well. If you pick up your children every evening at day care, for example, a job must provide you with regular, predictable hours and leave you with enough energy at the end of the day to fulfill the duties of your job as mother. You may need the flexibility to stay home with a sick child or to attend a special midday school event. These needs may shape your current career direction.

To find a career that suits you, consider your aspirations and what you enjoy. It is important to find a career that takes as much advantage as possible of your skills and your background. Look for the kind of work that allows interaction with people you like. If you enjoy talking to people, perhaps a career in sales will suit you. Is it important for you to be your own boss? Then perhaps you should start your own retail or service business. Don't be bound by the expectations of others. If a career as a teacher, an attorney, or a journalist doesn't appeal to you, consider investigating the real estate or construction industry.

Do you want a job that is challenging or exactingly routine? Would you like to be part of a team effort, or do you prefer to work alone? What kind of people do you enjoy being around, intellectuals or sometimes zany entrepreneurs? Review the following schedule of alternatives and see where you fit along the continuum.

PREDICTABLE ROUTINES	VARIED ROUTINES
Paperwork and reports	Constant contact with people
A single workplace	A great deal of travel
Undemanding work	Continuing challenges
A steady paycheck	Income that depends on what you produce
Steady security	Promotion or rejection
Being part of a team	Working alone
Contributing to society	Concentrating on profit or prestige
Exerting individual effort	Providing leadership

EDUCATION

◇ Decide what additional education you need, including formal classroom education, self-study programs, and on-the-job training. If your present education is sufficient, you are in luck. But if the career you are considering requires more training, investigate ways to obtain it. If you need a college degree, ask local colleges about available financial assistance, or the existence of night and weekend classes that would allow you to work and attend school simultaneously. If you lack particular job skills, such as computer training, determine which skills you can gain on the job as an apprentice or an intern, and which will require formal training. Then investigate the opportunities for obtaining it.

As a teenager, you were encouraged to pursue the education that would help you decide on a career. Now you must decide what career you want, and then secure the education that is appropriate to that career. Counselors at your local college can help you determine what education you need. A broad education that is appropriate to several different career directions may be more valuable to you than a narrow education that targets a specific career and does not allow for much latitude to change directions.

If you decide on additional formal training, make sure you select the appropriate school for your chosen field. For example, one woman who wanted to work in television broadcasting attended a seminar and met a local TV anchor, who told her that the local television station gave preference to interns from a particular technical school. This job seeker's choice of schools was then obvious. Be wary, however, of schools or institutes that advertise such connections. If you are told by a school's representative that it has a good record of placing students with certain companies, verify this information with the companies themselves before you accept it as fact.

Of course, no amount of training and education will ensure success unless you have an aptitude for the career you pursue. Be realistic about this. If you have little hand-eye coordination and your coordination cannot be significantly improved, rule out jobs that require a great deal of manual dexterity. If you are awkward with numbers and have tried without success to overcome your discomfort with math, a career as an accountant or a stockbroker will not suit you.

As you move toward a new career, your investigations may reveal qualities about your chosen career that you dislike. Don't be reluctant or embarrassed to change direction. Only by experimenting can you come to know what suits you. Whether you are trying to find a new career or improve an old one, don't give up your career search prematurely and settle for a job that does not employ your full potential. Finding career satisfaction is a process, and every step you take, even if it appears to be a misstep, is a move closer to your goals.

THE JOB SEARCH

◇ Your next step is to look for a job. Look in the classified section of your local newspaper, talk with friends and family about your objectives, contact professionals in your desired field, and call prospective employers. The more focused you are on your career desires, the easier it will be for you to find leads and follow them up.

Don't be shy; tell everyone you know that you are job hunting, and ask for their suggestions. You will be surprised at how many people you talk to may know someone who can help. If you are in school, consult the college placement office. If you are looking for a job in a particular industry, ask the professional association when a trade show or association conference will be held in your area. By attending such a show or conference, you will meet many people who will look at your résumé and give you suggestions. Nearly 80 percent of available jobs are not advertised, so you are most likely to find a job by talking with the right person or simply by being in the right place at the right time.

Visit a temporary placement agency and discuss the opportunities for temporary jobs available in the field you've chosen. As many as 10 to 20 percent of the people who start in temporary work are hired to stay on in permanent positions.

YOUR RÉSUMÉ

◇ Your résumé is a written advertisement for yourself. It is the history of your work experience and your individual accomplishments, and it may include references from former employers and professionals from your community. Look in your local library for guides for preparing a successful résumé.

Through your résumé, you have an opportunity to tell prospective employers who you are, what you would like to do for them, and what your past efforts, education, and experience can contribute to their organization. The experience you list on your résumé should include not only paying jobs, but also any volunteer work you have done. Emphasize your marketable skills and educational background. Your résumé should identify relevant work experience, including areas of responsibility, but you need not list salary figures. Likewise, the résumé should identify you, but need not provide information concerning your age, height and weight, marital status, children, or race.

CONSULTING A CAREER PROFESSIONAL

◇ You may consider employing a career professional in your job search. For a fee, three basic types of career professionals might help you find a job: personnel recruiters at employment agencies, career counselors, and executive recruiters.

Employment agencies The role of an employment agency is relatively straightforward. The agency solicits job orders from employers, seeks applicants to fill them, and then sends the applicants for interviews. Once the applicant is hired, the employment agency is paid a fee of 5 to 10 percent of the new employee's annual salary. Depending on local practice or agreement, the fee is paid by the applicant, by the employer, or split between the two.

Career counselors Career counselors are always paid by you, the job seeker. A career counselor will help you evaluate your skills and potential, prepare a résumé, and develop strategies for seeking employment. Since the counselor's job is to develop you as an applicant rather than find you specific placement, you pay a fee regardless of whether or not you find a job, and all or a portion of that fee will probably be paid in advance. Steer clear of high-priced career counselors who claim they have long-time connections with potential employers. Before you hire a career counselor, obtain references and check them. The career counselor should give you a formal contract that states exactly what services you will be provided and what the total cost will be for these services. The services you might expect include aptitude and psychological testing, drafting résumés, and training you for job interviews. You may be able to get these same services at a lesser cost or even free through your local community college.

The American Association for Counseling and Development offers a pamphlet titled "Selecting a Professional Counselor—The Choice Is Yours," which can be obtained by writing to the association at Department U, P.O. Box 9888, Alexandria, VA 22304. A list of certified career counselors in your area can be obtained by writing the National Board of Certified Counselors, 5999 Stevenson Avenue, Alexandria, VA 22304.

Executive recruiters Executive recruiters are sometimes called "headhunters." They are paid substantial fees by companies that are in the market for a candidate for a particular position, and they actively seek out potential applicants for these positions. If you are looking for a management or other executive position, or if you might be doing so in the future, contact a number of executive recruiters and let them know your qualifications. If you are just starting out in your field, most executive recruiters will not be interested in you. They are looking for prospects who are a known quantity with a demonstrated track record, and they prefer candidates who are currently employed in the industry in which they are seeking new employment.

THE JOB INTERVIEW

◇ You may decide to search for a job on your own. If you are sending your résumé to a company's personnel department but you are unsure of how to address it, call the company and ask the receptionist for the name, spelling, and title of the personnel department head. Then send your résumé with a cover letter introducing yourself. Briefly summarize your experience and education, and add that you will call for an appointment. Then follow up with a phone call and set a time for an interview.

Prepare for the interview by finding out as much as you can about the company and the people who work there. Talk to acquaintances who may be employed by the company. Read literature the company has published about its operations, and look for newspaper articles about the work it does. Study the job description for the position for which you are applying, so that you can be specific about telling the interviewer how your efforts will help the company attain its goals if you are hired.

On the day of the interview, dress appropriately for the job for which you are applying, and approach the interview with self-confidence. Remember that if you have done your homework, you will be better prepared for the job interview than most other candidates.

If you are an older woman who is reentering the job market, even if you have the necessary job skills you may feel at a disadvantage; as you wait for the interview, you will notice that the other applicants seem very, very young. Fortunately, many employers are beginning to regard maturity as an advantage. Studies have shown that older workers often are more stable and reliable, waste less time, exhibit more loyalty and responsibility, and require less supervision than younger workers. At your interview, emphasize your stability and maturity as assets, as well as your job skills.

Ask questions at your interview when you are given the opportunity. Find out what the job responsibilities are, how many people are in the department, what happened to the person you will be replacing (i.e., did he or she leave, get fired or promoted?), what kind of training you will receive, what the opportunities are for promotion, when you would start, and what kind of working hours are expected of you. Then discuss salary, benefits, and vacations.

Find out from the interviewer when the employer expects to make a hiring decision. Rarely will you be offered a job on the spot. After the interview, immediately write a thank-you note to the interviewer, reiterating your skills and telling the interviewer how interested you are—if you are—in the position ("After talking with you I am more interested than ever . . ."), and noting your belief that your skills will make you invaluable to the company. If you have not heard from the interviewer in what seems a reasonable amount of time, follow up the interview with a telephone call.

If you aren't hired for a job you want, talk with the interviewer about the reasons another candidate was chosen. Did that candidate have more education? More experience? Did the interviewer feel that the successful candidate would suit the company better than you would? Once you have established why you were not hired, you can assess the realities. Do you need more education or experience? Were you applying for a job that was not quite right for you? If you think this is the case, you might alter the focus of your job search slightly to overcome these obstacles. With each interview you will hone your interviewing skills and refine the focus of your search.

Pursue your job search methodically and carefully. Searching for a job is similar to dating, in that you interview a variety of potential mates, looking for the one who is uniquely right for you. As you pursue your job search, don't settle for just any job—keep looking until you find the one that fits your skills and interests.

FINANCIAL REWARDS

◇ If you are entering a new career, you will want to be paid the best entry-level salary possible, and to be assured that there is room for advancement, but you need experience before you can expect to be paid more. A prospective employer will consider what you can do for the company and what that contribution is worth. If your needs or desires exceed that amount, perhaps you should be looking for employment with a different company or in a different field.

Your salary will be based on two factors: what your work is worth to the employer, and what the employer has to pay to get you and keep you. To satisfy both factors, you must prove the value of your efforts and make clear your salary demands. To determine how much salary to ask for, you must know what others earn in comparable positions in other companies. Look at the classifieds, discreetly ask colleagues and associates, read salary surveys published by trade associations, and ask executive search firms about salary ranges for people in your position. Assess your own experience and capabilities, the current job market, and the opportunities for advancement. This will give you an idea of the range of salaries you might expect to be offered. If that range seems entirely too low, rethink your career objectives.

If you are currently employed, find out the salary ranges that your company uses, and where you fit within those ranges. If you are at the low end of the salary range for your position, find out what you must do to progress to the high end.

Don't necessarily choose the job that offers the highest salary. Money loses its luster if you are stuck in a job you dislike. You may find a job that pays well but offers very little opportunity for advancement. It may be a better career move to accept a position that pays less at the level at which you are entering but has unlimited future potential.

As you assess available positions, take special note of the benefits offered. Good medical insurance coverage is invaluable for a woman on her own, and a retirement plan can build security for your future that you cannot build on your own. If you are employed by a university, you and your family probably will be offered free or generously discounted courses. Indirect benefits are also important, such as a short commute, employee discounts, and generous vacations, holidays, and sick leave.

If your company offers outstanding medical, disability, and life insurance benefits and retirement plans, these programs may be worth far more to you than extra dollars in your paycheck. Value these benefits and add them to your salary to determine your true compensation. Other valuable fringe benefits include bonuses, expense accounts, dental insurance, club memberships, use of a company car, stock options, subscriptions, and union membership. Be sure to evaluate these benefits carefully when you are considering a job offer.

BEGINNING YOUR NEW JOB

◊ Once you are offered a job and you accept it, resolve to progress as rapidly as possible. Learn the details of your work and how best to accomplish them, and avoid the shoals of office politics and office gossip. Leave your personal problems at home. Display energy and enthusiasm, and perform your job as efficiently as possible. Work at top capacity. Be on time, try not to leave early, be judicious about the length of your lunch hours and coffee breaks, and avoid spending personal time on the telephone.

When you begin a new job, ask as many questions as you can without becoming intrusive, so you can learn what you need to know as rapidly as possible. Whenever you have a spare moment, you can learn a great deal by reviewing files. When you agree to have something done by a particular date, get it done on time. If you cannot meet a deadline, say so at the outset or as soon after it as possible, rather than risk appearing irresponsible if you are late.

If you become bored with routine, volunteer to take on other duties that might stimulate you. Create special projects that will further your company's goals. If you see a niche where you might be useful, sensitively demonstrate your potential value in such a way that the person whom you are helping need not feel threatened. Your enthusiasm and willingness to take on new tasks will impress your superiors, promote feelings of self-worth and accomplishment, and help you progress on the job.

Think creatively about your company and what you can contribute to its operations. Consider what you would do if you ran the company, then try to suggest practical and innovative ways to improve the company's products and market share. If you see an opportunity you think is being missed, or if you think of an improved product or service the company might offer, let management know about your ideas. Even if your suggestions are not implemented, your supervisors will realize that you are bright and interested in the goals and the success of the company. The hallmarks of a good employee are dependability, resourcefulness, good judgment, discretion, loyalty, objectivity, initiative, tact, and accuracy. Make all of these qualities yours.

MOVING ON

◊ If you find that you are not happy with your career, it is probably unwise to accept another job in the same field, even at a higher salary. It is likely that money is not your problem, and that you will be unhappy with the new job as well. Instead, carefully analyze why you are not satisfied with the job, and take steps to solve your dissatisfaction. If you like your company but are unhappy with your job, you may want to schedule an appointment with your superior to discuss the problems you are having. During the meeting, express your dissatisfaction carefully, and offer some suggestions or a range of possible solutions in a constructive discussion about how the situation might be improved.

If you cannot resolve matters positively, then prepare for leaving your job as carefully as you prepared for finding it. If you are considering changing jobs and you have a good health plan where you presently work, for example, get any needed medical and dental care for you and your family while you are still covered under the policy. That way, you won't risk incurring expenses while you are not employed, or when you are under a waiting period or an exclusion period for preexisting conditions in a new employer's medical plan. Remember also that under COBRA you can continue coverage under your present employer's health plan for 18 months.

If you decide to change jobs, timing may be critical. If there are only six months or a year before you become fully vested in your company's retirement plan, try to stay until you have satisfied that requirement. During this period, you can investigate other possibilities, take night courses in preparation for a job change, or take the opportunity to study on your own. While staying on a bit longer in a job you intend to leave may not be a bright prospect, the phase-out interlude may be very productive, and in retrospect you may find that it was the most practical way to make a job change.

When you leave a job, if you have vested pension benefits, you may receive a lump-sum distribution of these benefits. From the standpoint of tax planning and long-term retirement, it is probably to your advantage to roll those benefits into a tax-deferred IRA and invest them wisely. You will pay no tax on a lump-sum distribution if you roll it into an IRA within 60 days. (See chapter 8.)

GOING INTO BUSINESS FOR YOURSELF

◇ If you decide to undertake a business of your own, you will need an idea, a plan, and financial backing. Your business is unlikely to succeed without all three, and while most people who go into business start with an idea, most businesses that fail do so because they were undertaken without enough financing to sustain them through the period of becoming established. A solid business plan can tie the idea and the financing together to create a successful business.

A business plan is a blueprint for your company. It takes your business concept and turns it into a workable entity. The business plan will include a description of your business and the market for your product, identify your competition, describe your business structure, and outline your organization and personnel. It will include historical financial information, if any, project sales, expenses, and cash flow for three years; outline your marketing strategy, staffing, and equipment needs; and identify the source and amount of funding you expect, the application of that funding, and a break-even analysis.

You must arrange for adequate financing before you begin your new venture or you will surely fail. There are many ways of financing a business. You can use personal savings; borrow money from friends, family, or a financial institution; or take in a business partner to whom you give a share of the company in return for an investment in it. Your business plan will be a valuable tool when you seek capital funding, and it will also guide you as your business progresses. Revise your plan regularly as your business grows and develops, so you always have a good idea of where you intend to be going.

Once you have begun a business be sure to keep accurate financial records, so you have an up-to-the-minute account of where you stand and whether you are on target. Using this information, you can adjust your operations to meet your business and financial goals. If you find that your original business plan was unrealistic, you can make appropriate revisions. If those revisions reveal a need for additional financial backing, the sooner you know, the sooner you can begin to seek this additional financing.

If you go into business for yourself, you will have no one to report to, but you also must resign yourself to doing many jobs yourself because, at least at the beginning, there will be no one else to do them. You must be disciplined enough to be your own boss. If you lack the discipline to stay at work until the job is done, or the flexibility to be able to fulfill your work commitments before your personal and non-work life, you will be better off working for someone else.

Remember that entrepreneurs do not have anyone they can depend on for a regular paycheck. They must not only have faith in their undertaking, but also the character and financial resourcefulness to smooth out the bumps of an irregular income. A successful entrepreneur must have the discipline to save when the money comes in so that there will be funds available when it does not.

SELLING YOUR HOME

TO SELL OR NOT TO SELL?

◇ Many women find that continuing to own their family home is not the right decision after widowhood or divorce. Depending on personal preference, some women decide to free themselves from the financial responsibilities of mortgage payments, property taxes, and repairs. Others find simply that the house is larger than their diminished needs for housing. A large house may, indeed, be too much responsibility for a woman on her own, requiring substantial maintenance and upkeep when the time and money those demand might be far better spent elsewhere. Staying on in the same house may also hamper the gradual adjustment to a changed life and a new future.

The income taxes due on the sale of her home usually are not prohibitive for a widow, since the tax basis of the house will be established from the value it had at the date of her husband's death. While a substantial taxable gain might have been calculated had she and her husband sold the house prior to his death, she will have no taxable gain if she sells the house for that amount after he dies.

A divorced woman receives no similar tax break. If she accepts her home as a part of her property settlement, its tax basis carries over and is still established as the amount that she and her husband paid for the house—and sometimes less, if they had deferred a gain from a prior home sale under the residence replacement provisions of the Internal Revenue Code. If she decides to sell the house after the divorce, she will owe a great deal of income tax, unless she replaces the house with one that costs at least as much as the net sales price of the former house. As most women on their own again are scaling down the size of their living quarters along with their expenses, this is often not a practical alternative.

If you are divorcing and you allow your husband to have the house by buying your share, you will escape these tax and reinvestment problems. Before you agree to this arrangement, be aware that on average, men remarry within two years of having been divorced. If you believe that it will trouble you if your ex-husband sets up house-keeping with a new partner in your former home, then you may want to decide that the house be sold now.

If you no longer want to live in your home, but you consider it a good investment, you may want to rent it rather than sell it. Renting it for enough to cover costs may be economically sound, but tenants may not maintain it as well as you do. As a landlord, you will encounter other problems as well. Explore these questions carefully:

- Will a responsible tenant be easy to find?
- If the tenant decides to move, could it be difficult to find another one?
- If the property is vacant for a month or more, do you have the finances to cover the mortgage payment while you are seeking a new tenant?
- Will you be able to manage the property on your own, or will you need to retain a professional management company to take over?

If you want to continue living in your home but cannot afford the payments and the upkeep, you have several options. You can rent a room or two to a tenant in a house-sharing arrangement. If you are over 62, you can tap the equity in your home through a reverse mort-gage that pays you each month. A second job also may enable you to keep the house, but after all the years you toiled to maintain your fam-ily and support their needs, do you really want to continue to make sacrifices for your home now? Consider the pros and cons carefully before you decide whether keeping the house at this stage of your life merits the sacrifices that may be required to do so.

If the only way to divide the property or settle the estate is to sell the house, choice is a luxury you may not have.

CHOOSING A REAL ESTATE AGENT

◇ A real estate agent or broker is hired by the seller to find a buyer and help negotiate a fair purchase price. Most real estate agencies, whether large or small, have access to listings for most of the properties for sale in their areas through the Multiple Listing Service (MLS). If one broker lists the property for sale and another finds a buyer, the brokers will split the commission.

To choose the real estate agent with whom you will list your property, ask friends and neighbors for recommendations, and knock on the doors of homes for sale in your neighborhood to ask the owners about their experiences with their listing agents. You are seeking an agent who will aggressively market your property, advertise it, and hold open houses with the purpose of attracting as many potential buyers as possible, as well as other brokers who might bring their own clients. The agent should be familiar with the housing market in your area, and particularly with your neighborhood and your type of home. Your agent should be willing to cooperate with other brokers and list your property in the Multiple Listing Service. Interview a number of agents, but do not select an agent on the basis of the price at which the agent agrees to list your property. Your real concern should be the price at which the property will be sold, not an unrealistically high price that an agent might propose only to obtain your listing and then later reduce substantially. Ask the agent to furnish you with the sales price, the original asking price, and the number of months on the market for other houses for which she or he was the listing agent. Such a list will tell you whether the agent is accustomed to quoting a very high listing price to secure listings and then persuading the seller to lower the price a few months later.

Real estate agents are paid by commission, usually 6 percent of the sales price. That commission is always paid by the seller at the time of closing, and it is reasonable if your agent does a good job and secures the best price possible for the property. In most cases it is not wise to negotiate with the broker at the outset for a lower commission; the agent will be eager to sell properties with the highest commissions and may not market your property as aggressively as you would like, nor will other brokers be as interested in showing a low-commission property as a full-commission property. After you have received an offer, the listing agent may be willing to negotiate for a lower commission as a way of bringing buyer and seller together. Assume, for example, that you have listed your house at $200,000 and have said you will not accept less than $190,000. If you receive an offer of $187,000 from a buyer who will pay no more than that, your broker may agree to a reduction in commission to secure the deal.

When you decide to list your house with a real estate agent, you sign a listing agreement that spells out your rights and obligations. The listing will usually run for about three months and will grant the real estate agency an exclusive right to sell your property; it will also provide that the house be listed in the MLS. Usually, your broker will receive a commission no matter who finds the buyer for the house during the listing period—plus any renewals—even if it is you. If you do not renew the listing and it expires, you will still have to pay a commission if you sell the house to someone who first saw it during the listing period. If you want to list your house with a real estate agent but you know of someone who may be interested in buying it, list your prospect as an exception in the written broker's agreement. If they decide to buy it, you will not have to pay a broker's commission on the sale.

FOR SALE BY OWNER

◇ You may consider selling your house yourself, and then advertising it and erecting a For Sale by Owner sign in your front yard or window. Proceeding in this way may save a considerable amount in commissions, but you should be aware of the potential problems in store:

Problem #1. Setting the price for your home.
Solution #1. If you do not obtain a professional appraisal to justify
    the price you set, ask a local real estate agent for a listing of com-

parable recently sold houses in your neighborhood, known as a "market analysis."

Problem #2. Qualifying the buyer, to find out whether potential buyers can actually afford your house.

Solution #2. At your local stationer or office supply store you can purchase an application form to be completed by potential buyers, requesting financial information about their income, the source of the down payment they will make, and their plans about paying cash, obtaining mortgage financing, etc.

Problem #3. Real estate agents on your doorstep who see your For Sale by Owner sign and promise an interested buyer if you will sign a listing contract.

Solution #3. Offer to sign a contract only for a named buyer. In that way, the agent will get a commission if he or she brings that buyer to you, but you need not pay a commission if the house is sold to a buyer you find.

Problem #4. Bargain shoppers. If your house is for sale by owner, a prospective buyer may offer you a relatively low amount, knowing you are saving a 6 percent commission.

Solution #4. If your asking price is fair, hold out for a qualified buyer at your price.

Problem #5. Advertising. Unless you use an agent, you will probably not have access to the Multiple Listing Service, and you must pay for your own advertising expenses, which can be substantial.

Solution #5. Look into the possibility of locating an agency that belongs to MLS and will agree to help you sell and advertise your property for a fixed fee.

Problem #6. Doorbell ringing day and night. Passersby who notice your sign may want to look through your house at inconvenient times.

Solution #6. Make sure your For Sale by Owner sign says By Appointment Only, a measure that will lessen your problem but will still not entirely alleviate it.

Problem #7. Your advertising attracts far fewer potential buyers than a real estate broker could supply.

Solution #7. You may decide that paying a commission is worth it, and turn to a broker.

TIMING

◇ Whether or not you use a broker, don't make the very common mistake of assuming that your home will be sold only a month or two after you have put it on the market, and consequently buy a new home before selling the old one. Unless you have paid cash, you will be making double mortgage payments and stretching your financial resources to the limit. You might be able to rent your old home while it is on the market, but few renters want strangers looking through their home or to know that the place might be sold from under them at any time. If you have been transferred or otherwise must leave your old home and buy a new one elsewhere, you may have no choice. But if you have options, it is far wiser to continue to live in your old home until it is sold. Remember, too, that the sale of a home is not final until the closing. Real estate brokers have many tales to tell about deals that have not closed even after substantial down payments have been made. Keep your expectations at a moderate level until the sale has been consummated.

Certain income tax benefits are available to you when you sell your home. If you sell your principal residence and replace it within two years by purchasing a residence of at least equal value, you may defer paying taxes on any gains. And if you sell your principal residence after reaching age 55, you can make a one-time election to exclude up to $125,000 of gain from the sale if you have lived in the house for three out of the previous five years. Be sure to consult your accountant about your particular tax situation before assuming that these provisions will apply to you.

PAYING INCOME TAX

Income tax preparation is sometimes particularly daunting for women who have been recently divorced or widowed. They confront new tax filing statuses, rules for claiming exemptions for children, and special provisions regarding alimony, child support, Social Security benefits, pension benefits, insurance proceeds, child-care expenses, legal fees, medical expenses, and estate administration costs.

INCOME TAX RATES

◇ American income tax tables are progressive, which means that as one's income increases, each successive layer is subject to a higher tax rate. If, therefore, you assume that the very rich pay tax at a much higher tax rate than the rest of us, you are wrong. For the single taxpayer, the top tax bracket of 31 percent begins at a taxable income level of about $52,000. For a married couple the 31 percent tax bracket begins at $86,500. All income above that level is taxed at the maximum tax rate, so if your taxable income is $52,000 ($86,500 if married), no one in the country pays tax at a higher rate than you do. While this seems unfair, it also maximizes your opportunities for deduction. Every deduction you find and any income that is excludable from taxes will reduce your tax payments. To manage your money successfully, you must learn exactly what is taxable and what is not, and which expenses you can properly deduct.

YOUR FILING STATUS

◇ Each filing status has its own rules and tax rates. If you are unmarried or legally separated with no children at home, your filing status is "Single." If you maintain a home for a child or another dependent, your status is "Head of Household." If you are widowed, you can file as "Married Filing Jointly" for the year of your husband's death, and as "Qualifying Widow" for the next two years, if you have a dependent child and you do not remarry. If you are currently married, you will probably file as "Married Filing Jointly," although you may instead file a return of your own as "Married Filing Separately." If you and your husband have not lived together for the last six months of the year, and you have dependent children, you may file as "Head of Household," even though you are still married. (This provision originally was enacted to benefit abandoned spouses, but it may benefit you even though you have not been abandoned.)

If your filing status is "Single," you must file a tax return if your income is at least $5,900. If you are "Head of Household," you must file a tax return if your gross income is over $7,550. As a "Qualifying Widow," you needn't file unless your income is over $8,300, and if you are "Married Filing Jointly," your combined income must exceed $10,600 before you are required to file. If you are "Married Filing Separately," you must file a tax return if your income is over $2,300.

You are entitled to deduct an exemption of $2,300 for yourself and for each of your dependent children on your tax return. Your children are your dependents if you had physical custody of them for the greatest number of days of the year, unless your divorce decree grants the exemption to your ex-husband and you sign a Form 8332 to be attached to his tax return. If you were divorced before 1985 and your divorce decree grants the exemptions for your children to your ex-husband, he may claim the dependency exemptions if he provided at least $600 of support for them.

As noted earlier, your husband may want to claim the dependency exemptions for your children even though you have physical custody. This is why it is important that in negotiating a divorce you insist upon a clause in your marital settlement agreement that says you will sign Form 8332, which allows him to claim the exemptions only if his child support payments for the year have been made in full and on time. Because the majority of child support payments are not paid on time, and are often not paid at all, this added incentive for timely payments may be of great benefit to you. Signing Form 8332 will not affect your ability to claim deductions for other expenses for your child, such as medical payments or child-care credit.

Dependency exemptions cannot be split in half. If you and your former spouse decide to share the dependency exemptions for your three children, for example, one of you can claim two exemptions and the other one, or one of you can claim all three exemptions, but the exemptions cannot be otherwise divided.

Your husband may request the dependency exemptions for your children even though they will not reduce his taxes under current tax law. Under phaseout provisions, a taxpayer loses 2 percent of the dependency exemptions for each $2,500 that his or her income exceeds $100,000. If your husband's income exceeds $222,500, the dependency exemptions will do him no good at all, and they should be shifted to your tax return to reap the greatest tax savings.

TAX TREATMENT
OF ALIMONY AND CHILD SUPPORT

◊ Child support payments are not taxable to you, but alimony (sometimes called family support, spousal support, spousal maintenance, et cetera) is included in your taxable income if it meets all of the criteria we noted earlier. (See chapter 5.)

If you receive taxable alimony, you are allowed to make a tax-deductible contribution of up to $2,000 to an IRA—if you otherwise qualify for an IRA deduction.

If your alimony is reduced by more than $15,000 over the first three years after your divorce, at the end of the third year you should make the recapture computation that is set forth in the tax code. The computed recapture amount will be a deduction for you in that year and taxable to your ex-husband.

To keep your ex-husband from disguising nondeductible child support payments as deductible alimony, the law provides that if alimony payments are scheduled to decrease at the time your child turns 18, 21, or the locally designated age of majority, the amount of the reduction will be considered to be nondeductible child support. The same will be true if the payment is set to decrease upon a contingency related to the child, such as the child's moving away from home, marrying, obtaining employment, et cetera. The rules are complex, so if your situation is such that you might be affected, consult a qualified tax professional.

Although the property divided in a divorce is not taxable, there are hidden tax consequences. For example, if you accept property that has become valuable after you and your husband paid a relatively modest amount for it, you will owe tax on considerable capital gains when you sell it. If you receive your family home as a portion of your settlement and subsequently sell it, you will pay substantial taxes on the gain unless you buy a new home of equivalent value within two years, or unless you qualify for the once-in-a-lifetime exclusion of $125,000 for those who are 55 or older and who have lived in the home for three of the five years prior to its sale. Consult a tax professional about the tax consequences of this situation before negotiating such a settlement. (See chapter 5.)

SOCIAL SECURITY BENEFITS

◇ If you are receiving Social Security benefits, half of those benefits will be taxable if your total annual income, including tax-free income, exceeds $25,000 ($32,000 on a joint tax return).

THE STANDARD DEDUCTION

◇ If you cannot claim many deductions, the government allows you a standard tax deduction of $3,600 if you are single ($5,250 for head of household and $6,000 on a joint return). If your itemized deductions do not exceed that amount, you will claim this standard deduction on your tax return instead of itemizing the deductions. If you are at least 65 years old or you are blind, your standard deduction is increased by $850 if you are single or $650 if you are married.

LEGAL FEES

◇ Legal and professional fees you pay for tax planning are deductible if your miscellaneous deductions exceed 2 percent of your adjusted gross income. If you divorce, a portion of the legal fees you pay may be deductible as well. Legal fees that you pay "for the production of income" are deductible if they are stated separately. For example, if your $200-an-hour attorney spent four hours negotiating a favorable alimony provision for you, the $800 legal fee will be tax-deductible. If your property settlement includes rental property, stocks, or other investments, the fees spent to secure that property for you can be deducted when you sell the investment. Ask your attorney to analyze your bill and to itemize the expenses separately. The attorney may charge you a small fee of $25 or so for doing this, but the tax deduction will probably be worth it.

HOME MORTGAGE INTEREST

◇ If you are financially able to do so, consider paying off your home mortgage rather than keeping the money in the bank. If your home mortgage is at 10 percent and current certificates of deposit are earning only 8 percent, paying off the mortgage would be the equivalent of investing your money at 10 percent rather than at 8 percent.

By paying off your mortgage you will lose the interest deduction claimed on your tax forms, but you will still be better off. Consider these figures: If you owe $50,000 on your home mortgage at 10 percent interest, you pay $5,000 of interest each year. At a 30 percent tax bracket, that $5,000 deduction saves you $1,500 a year in income taxes, so your net after-tax interest cost is $3,500. To pay off the mortgage, you would have to use $50,000 of your savings. If that $50,000 is invested at 8 percent, it is earning $4,000 a year in taxable interest income. At your 30 percent tax rate, the tax is $1,200, leaving you $2,800 after taxes. By paying off your mortgage, you are losing income of $2,800 after taxes, but saving $3,500 in interest, which puts you $700 ahead, year after year. You should not, of course, consider paying off your home mortgage with funds that are earmarked for a specific purpose in the near future, such as a child's education, your living expenses, or an emergency fund.

Since the interest paid on automobile loans is not tax-deductible, your savings will be even more dramatic if you use money from your savings to buy a new car rather than financing it. To replenish your savings, find out how much payments would have been and make monthly payments to your savings or investment accounts rather than to the financial institution. You will end up many dollars ahead.

JOB-HUNTING EXPENSES

◊ You are not permitted to claim a tax deduction for expenses incurred in looking for your first job, or after you have been unemployed for a long period. But if you are looking for new employment in your same line of work, you are permitted to deduct all expenses, regardless of whether you find employment as a result of the expenditures. These job-hunting expenses include travel and auto expenses, résumé preparation, mailing, printing, et cetera, and they are deductible as miscellaneous itemized deductions after you subtract 2 percent of your adjusted gross income from the total miscellaneous deductions.

If you combine a vacation with a job search, only the expenses that relate to the job search are deductible, but if the sole purpose of the trip was job hunting, the entire trip is deductible.

EDUCATIONAL EXPENSES

◊ You may deduct the cost of all education you acquire to maintain or improve your existing job skills or to meet the express requirements of your employer to keep your job. You may not deduct the educational expenses you may incur to meet the minimum requirements for your job, or to qualify you for a new job. For example, if you work as a paralegal, you may deduct courses in which you learn more about law, but you may not deduct the expenses of attending law school, since these will qualify you for a new job as an attorney. Educational expenses, including tuition, books, fees, travel, professional dues, magazine subscriptions, et cetera, are deductible only if you itemize your deductions, and they are subject to the 2-percent floor.

Travel in connection with an educational pursuit is deductible, but travel simply as a form of education is not. For example, a professor of Spanish literature will not be permitted to deduct a sightseeing trip through Spain, but a trip to Spain to do specific research in the libraries there is deductible so long as it can be substantiated.

Even if your educational expenses are not currently deductible, your expenditures for books may be deductible in the future. For example, the books that you buy during law school will be useful to you in your law practice. You may be able to depreciate your library costs once you begin working if you can substantiate these costs, so it is important to keep track of such expenditures for professional books. Ask your tax adviser for more specific guidance.

WHAT TO CLAIM ON YOUR W-4 FORM

◊ Your employer withholds income taxes from your paycheck in accordance with the W-4 form you prepare. The more allowances you claim, the less tax will be withheld. You should claim withholding allowances for yourself and any dependent children, and claim special allowances for total itemized deductions. If you indicate that you are single, more taxes will be withheld than if you are married. If you are divorcing and expect the divorce to be final by the end of the year, fill out a new W-4 form as soon as possible, indicating single marital status.

The Internal Revenue Service requires that you pay 90 percent of your tax during the year or 100 percent of your previous year's taxes, so if you have alimony income or other income not subject to withholding, you will be penalized if you do not pay taxes on that income during the year. You may ask your employer to take additional taxes out of your paycheck, or you may file quarterly estimated tax forms. To figure the extra amount your employer should withhold or that you should pay in estimated tax, jot estimates of your income and deductions for the current year in the margin of last year's tax return, and figure the tax. Divide that amount by 12, subtract your current monthly withholding for federal income taxes, and the difference is the additional monthly amount you should ask your employer to withhold. If you choose to file estimated tax forms instead, obtain these forms from the Internal Revenue Service and pay one-fourth of your estimated annual tax with each quarterly form on April 15, June 15, September 15, and January 15. Claim credit on your tax return for the amount withheld from your paycheck plus any estimated tax payments you have made. If you have computed your estimated tax correctly, the balance due, if any, will be very small.

CREATING CREDIT ON YOUR OWN

◇ Few people can live conveniently today without credit, secured or unsecured. Credit that is secured by a lien against your real estate, automobiles, or other property is referred to as secured credit, with your property as the collateral. Unsecured credit includes charge accounts, credit cards, and signature loans. Most of us need credit at some time or other—to buy a new house, a new car, to make home improvements, or to cope with emergencies. For better or for worse, we live in a society built on credit, and establishing credit is often an obstacle to newly single women.

Women, particularly those who are divorcing, often have a more difficult time obtaining credit than men do. Financial institutions may not discriminate on the basis of sex or marital status, but in determining whether to grant you credit they can, by law, assess not only your willingness to repay, but what is, in their perception, your ability to repay. Simply having a good credit rating does not mean you will be granted credit. A good credit history demonstrates your willingness to repay, but you may not be able to satisfy a credit institution's standards for whether you have the ability to repay as well.

Women still earn less than men, and, consequently, are generally perceived as having a lesser ability to repay. Credit institutions regard with special scrutiny the divorcing woman who receives alimony and child support under temporary orders. Since such orders are subject to change when the divorce is final, lenders often refuse to consider that temporary income as reliable. In addition, they may determine that your debt-to-income ratio is too high. Even though your husband may be making the mortgage payment on your family home, if it is your joint legal obligation, the full mortgage payment will be considered as your debt. If your own earnings are not sufficient to support your entire joint obligations, you will probably not be able to obtain new credit cards, an auto loan, or a mortgage for a new home.

If you are divorcing and the credit cards you have were granted in your husband's name, with your name listed as an additional, secondary cardholder, your husband can ask that your name be deleted and your card no longer honored. Under the Equal Credit Opportunity Act, creditors cannot automatically cancel an account when your marital status changes, but they are allowed to eliminate the secondary card. As discussed previously, if your credit was granted in your husband's name, apply now for credit in your own name, so your credit cards will not be revoked when you are later divorced or widowed. A creditor also may require reapplication for credit cards and charge accounts because of a change in your marital status if the credit was originally based on income earned by your husband, and if your income at the time of the original application would not support your current debt.

A lender is required to include alimony and child support in its determination of whether to grant you credit if it is determined that the payments are likely to be consistently received in the future. The creditor may consider such factors as court decrees, the length of time you have been receiving the payments, the regularity of your receipt, the procedures available to compel payment, such as wage garnishment, and the payor's credit worthiness. If you are receiving alimony or child support, be prepared to prove that you receive the payments regularly by showing copies of the checks, deposits, or a statement by your former husband. If you cannot prove that you receive alimony and child support on a regular basis, you will probably be better off not mentioning these payments as a source of income.

If you are retired, your retirement income, including Social Security, pension, disability, and welfare payments, must be counted as income by potential creditors. A credit institution is not allowed to discriminate against you on account of your age or your ineligibility for credit life insurance, as it is illegal to require insurance as a condition of getting credit. (See chapter 2.)

MANAGING AN INHERITANCE OR A SETTLEMENT

Wealth can be both a blessing and a burden. Because what seems like a great deal of money to one person may be a relatively modest sum to someone else, any amount of money that is greater than what you are accustomed to dealing with can present new money management questions.

After the death of your husband, you may receive a substantial life insurance settlement and be faced for the first time with deciding how to manage your estate. Or you may receive an insurance settlement for a casualty loss, an award for a personal injury claim, or a divorce settlement. Perhaps you have inherited money from a parent or another relative, or realized a large profit on your work or in an investment. No matter what the source of such money, you will probably have to address both emotional and investment factors as you decide how to manage it.

If you are accustomed to not having much money and have prided yourself on being able to live on very little, you may be surprised to find that you feel ashamed of your sudden wealth. If the amount of money you have acquired thrusts you into a different social status, such an experience can make you feel like an imposter. Sometimes money can make you angry, particularly if you relinquished something you valued highly, or suffered great pain before receiving it. Its source can be a major factor in how you regard this relative wealth, and, given the wide range of possible emotional reactions its arrival can evoke, the first thing you should do is—nothing. Put the money into a separate account where it will earn a reasonable rate of interest, such as in a money market fund, and do nothing more to spend or invest it until you are in a settled frame of mind to plan your strategy.

MAKING PLANS

◇ While you are coming to terms with your new wealth, begin to make some plans. Decide how much of the money is for pleasure and how much you would like to invest. Allocate a certain amount for spending, based on your needs for the future. If this money is the only inheritance you expect to receive, you will want to preserve a great deal of it. If, however, you will be receiving a payment each year for the rest of your life, then investing for the future is far less important. Consider your personal situation as you decide how much you can reasonably spend now.

Once you have decided how much you can spend immediately, it is time to decide how you will spend it. A spending spree may easily lead to exhausting what you have allocated, and you might be forced to tap reserved investment funds to satisfy your immediate desires.

Make an impulse list of everything you want to buy and the amount each item will cost. Add to this list, over several weeks, jotting down everything you think you would really like to do or acquire. After a month or so, carefully review the list. For certain items, you will find that simply listing them as possibilities you could now afford was pleasure enough, and now you can easily cross them off the list. Identify other items you might indeed want to have in the future, but will not pursue now, cross these off the list as well and put them on a new list itemizing future purchases. As you cull this impulse list, you will find yourself approaching spending in a less precipitate manner, weighing the cost and the attractiveness of the item against your needs and satisfaction. Once you have pared down the list to the items you really want and feel comfortable about buying, go ahead and spend the money. You will find this measured approach more enriching and satisfying than the kind of impulsive spending that leaves you worried that you might have overspent, uneasy about having indulged your whims, and unsatisfied because the intense spending period has come to an end.

INVESTING

◇ Now turn your attention to the money you have set aside for your future. Make a list of the specific financial goals you would like to accomplish with this money, and methods of accomplishing them. If you have come into vast sums, you will have plenty of money to fulfill your needs, but chances are that your money will not be enough to fund all of your financial goals. As you did with the impulse list, decide which financial goals may not be sufficiently important and which goals can be modified or put off to reconsider or pursue at a later date. Perhaps certain of the financial goals can be accomplished in part, or on a relatively smaller scale than you first contemplated. For example, if you would like to buy an expensive new home and also send your teenager to a high-priced college, you may not have enough money to do both. Perhaps you will decide on a less costly house, or your child will attend a less expensive university. If your child is younger, you can set money aside for a portion of his or her education and add to the fund each month from current earnings. Weighing the alternatives for each of your financial goals will allow you to place them in perspective.

After you have set specific financial goals for your money, you will be able to allocate your assets accordingly. Pay particular attention to your time frame and to your ability to tolerate risk. When you invest money that you will be needing to use soon for a specific purpose, such as a child's education or an automobile purchase, you may not want to endure the ups and downs of the stock market. (See chapter 4.) Instead, choose a certificate of deposit or a U.S. Treasury or corporate bond that will mature at the time you need the money. If you are investing for your retirement, and it is still many years away, you need not limit your investments to certificates of deposits and bonds. Over the long term, a diversified stock portfolio will probably yield a far greater return and result in much higher retirement income for you.

If you do not already consult a particular financial adviser, you may wish to do so now. Even if you have inherited an enormous amount of money, safety is paramount, since you will probably not be able to regenerate that money if you suffer severe losses in risky investments. If you are usually an aggressive risk-taker, you need to curb these tendencies and manage the money in a moderate mode to preserve your capital. (See chapter 4.)

RETIREMENT

The combination of Social Security, company pensions, IRAs, Keogh plans, and other retirement plans now provides American retirees with more benefits than were ever available before. Nevertheless, legislative changes have caused many companies to reduce pension funding, and since the Tax Reform Act of 1986, many small pension plans have been frozen and contributions to qualified employee savings plans have been sharply curtailed. The stability of many pension plans has been a matter of great concern in recent years. And while the Social Security system is solid, some legislators want to use the Social Security surplus to fund current budgetary spending, rather than reserving it for the retirement of the current and future work force.

For the most part, it is men who are covered by pensions and retirement plans. Pension benefits for women average only $417 per month compared with $744 a month for men, and 80 percent of women who are now of retirement age have no pension.

No matter how old you are now, it is important for you to take steps to plan for your retirement. People are living longer than ever before in history. If you began working at age 22 and retire at age 65, chances are that you will live for as many years in retirement as you did before you began working full-time. Unless you plan now, inflation will be a serious obstacle to the standard of living you expect to be able to maintain during your retirement years.

In the past 20 years, inflation has careened from nearly 0 to 18 percent, and has averaged 6.5 percent per year. At that rate prices double every 12 years; if you retire at age 65, by the time you are 77, everything will cost twice as much as it did when you retired. If you live to be 90, costs will have doubled again, and on your one-hundredth birthday, prices will be eight times as high as when you retired 35 years earlier.

Inflation is here to stay. In 1971, the Nixon administration imposed wage and price controls because of "dangerous inflationary conditions" of 3.7 percent. With the current figure under 5 percent, politicians tell us that inflation is under control. Given the obvious shift in expectations regarding the presence of inflation, it would be unrealistic to believe that inflation will ever approach 0 percent again. It is imperative that you plan inflation into your retirement program to ensure that you limit the damage it will otherwise mean for your personal standard of living years from now.

THE SOCIAL SECURITY SYSTEM

Many people believe that the Social Security system is meant to provide for American retirement, an assertion that is not true. The Social Security system was intended to provide a basic floor on which Americans can build for their retirement. Unfortunately, many retirees end up living on nothing but Social Security income, and a meager existence it is.

The Social Security system was created as a pay-as-you-go plan, not an endowment plan of cash reserves to pay benefits in the future. The early recipients of Social Security will collect far more than they ever paid into the system, but this is far from the case for the generation born after World War II. A husband and wife born in 1945 who each earn $25,000 a year will pay about $124,000 more in Social Security taxes than they will ever collect in benefits, according to the Center for Economic Policy at Stanford University.

PLANNING YOUR RETIREMENT

Planning for your retirement requires four steps:

1. Predict your retirement expenses.
2. Predict your retirement income.
3. Compute the retirement savings you need.
4. Make economic and actuarial assumptions.

Predict Your Retirement Expenses. Your retirement expenses depend on a number of factors:

1. When will you retire?
2. Do you plan to work for as long as you are able, or to retire earlier? This will have an impact on how much you will spend during retirement.
3. Do you plan to be active, traveling extensively, for example, or will you settle into a retirement community and be content with the social and cultural life of your general area?
4. Where will you live? Will you own or rent your home? What will your housing costs be? What debts will you owe at retirement?
5. How much will your health care cost?
6. What will your income tax situation be?

Predict Your Retirement Income. Most people need income from investments in order to retire completely, or else they must go on working to supplement retirement plans and Social Security. To predict your retirement income, answer these questions:

1. Will you work part-time during retirement?
2. Are you building investments, or will some of your current investments be spent before retirement?
3. How much will you receive from pension plans, Social Security, and other retirement plans? These amounts form the base upon which your other retirement income will build.
4. Which of your investments can be spent during retirement,

and which do you want to keep intact to pass on to your survivors?

Computing the Retirement Savings You Need. Most financial planners advocate perpetuity planning, assuming that if you need $50,000 each year to live on and your investments earn an average of 10 percent, you will need a $500,000 nest egg that will produce $50,000 of income each year. But why, you might ask, should your income go on forever when you won't? Certainly it makes more sense to plan to deplete assets in order to support your standard of living. That way you will not need to accumulate as much during your lifetime, and you will have more disposable income after retirement. The financial planners who advocate this kind of precise planning—as opposed to perpetuity planning—advise depleting one's principal through regular withdrawals during one's lifetime. Because those who adopt precise planning have to hope that they will expire before their capital reaches zero, moderating between these extreme alternatives seems to be the best course.

Make Economic and Actuarial Assumptions. The solution to the extremes posed by perpetuity planning and precise planning lies in the actuarial assumptions you make for your own retirement planning. Plan your finances as though you will live to be 100. If you die earlier, your survivors will inherit more. Assume that you will need about 75 percent of your preretirement income in retirement. If the amount seems small, remember that while you may plan to travel, you will not be commuting to work regularly or spending as much on clothing or other such business-related expenses. Inflation is unpredictable, so you should not attempt to project inflation figures during your retirement years. Instead, simply assume that you will have to earn about 3 percent over inflation on your investments, and use that 3 percent figure in your planning.

RETIREMENT PLANNING WORKSHEET

◇ To compute the amount you must save each year to meet your retirement needs (see Appendix D), take the additional amount needed to fund retirement on line 10, part 3, and multiply it by the annual savings factor from the chart below:

YEARS UNTIL RETIREMENT	ANNUAL SAVINGS FACTOR
5	.188
10	.087
15	.054
20	.037
25	.027
30	.021

The result of your multiplication is the amount you must save each year between now and retirement to meet your retirement goals.

How to Meet a Shortfall

◇ If the annual savings you have computed is more than you can manage, there are several ways in which you can attempt to meet the shortfall:

1. Increase the rate of return on your existing investments. Remember, the retirement planning information supplied assumes that you will be earning 3 percent over inflation on your investments. Perhaps you might reposition your investments so that you earn more. Remember, however, that the greater the potential earnings, the greater the risk, so this may not be the proper alternative for you to pursue.

2. Instead of increasing the rate of return on existing investments, you can leave them intact, and increase the rate of return on the new investments that you make. This way, you would still be increasing your risk, but only on a portion of your investment portfolio.

3. Increase the amount of money that you can save by taking on another job or by decreasing your current expenses.

4. Consider changing some of your actuarial assumptions. The information supplied here assumes that you will live to be 100. Perhaps your family health and mortality history makes

this a grossly unrealistic assumption. If you believe that you will probably not need to plan for extreme longevity, you might decide to deplete your capital at a faster rate during retirement.

5. If your children will help support you in your old age, you need not provide all of your retirement support yourself. (Some women who have married affluent men late in life and assume they will be sufficiently supported through their retirement find that their husbands die long before they do and pass on all their assets to their surviving children.)

6. Reduce inflation risk before you retire by locking in fixed-rate mortgages, buying appliances and other assets that probably will not need replacing during your lifetime, or otherwise reducing your anticipated future expenditures.

HOW TO INCREASE
ANNUAL SAVINGS AND INVESTMENTS

◇ All it takes to increase your savings is discipline, which you can muster sufficiently if you really believe you need to save more. To gain that discipline, think critically about every expenditure you make.

You might find it easier to increase your savings if you do so gradually. If you are currently saving nothing, start now to save $5 a day, which is $150 a month. Next year, increase that amount by more, perhaps to $6 or $7 a day, and the year after a bit more than that. Making gradual increases will not be nearly as difficult as trying to save $1,000 a month right now.

Taxes of any sort are a drain on the budget, and reducing your taxes will directly allow you to increase the amounts you save. If you are in a high tax bracket, perhaps a tax-free or tax-deferred investment would work for you. Increasing the amount you invest in your tax-deferred retirement plan is better than increasing the amount that goes to your savings account, if the money will be used for retirement anyway.

Perhaps you can reduce your living expenses. Or perhaps you can combine a reduction of living expenses with an increase in income, by finding a job that gives you better wages or benefits than you are now receiving, by taking on a second job, or by turning what is presently a hobby into an income-producing activity. Perhaps you can take slightly more risks with your money by using other people's money to earn money, as you probably did when you bought your home, investing the bank's money along with yours. As discussed previously, if your children are older but still living with you, perhaps they can contribute toward household expenses, enabling you to save a bit more for your retirement.

WHAT TO DO WITH AN EXCESS

◇ If your retirement-planning calculations show you are actually saving more than you need, you will end up with more money than you need in retirement. If that is your situation, you have several options. You can reduce the risk level for your invested assets, reducing the rate of return and increasing the safety element. Or perhaps you might save less and allow yourself to spend more money on current expenses and luxuries.

If that doesn't suit you, you can begin giving money away, either to charity or to help family members now, rather than leaving a large amount of money to them when you die.

MEDICAL INSURANCE

In the years since the Medicare program was first introduced, Medicare coverage has been sharply curtailed. Cost containment has become the byword, and the Medicare reimbursement schedule does not cover the full cost of most medical procedures. There are so many gaps in Medicare coverage today that additional medical insurance coverage is essential.

If you are over 65, you are probably eligible for the two-part Medicare program. Part A automatically covers in-patient hospital bills after you have paid a deductible of $658 each year. Once you pay the deductible, most hospital bills are entirely covered under Part A. Part B is optional and covers medical expenses incurred out of the hospital, such as physician services, outpatient services, lab fees, ambulance services, and outpatient psychiatric care. Though 80 percent of the Medicare premium's allowable physician fees are covered under Part B, with the patient paying the other 20 percent, the patient must also pay all physician fees in excess of the allowable charge. While Medicare has reduced or frozen the amount of these fees that they reimburse, excess doctor charges have escalated dramatically. Unless you have other medical coverage, such as military health benefits, you should accept the optional Part B coverage, and consider additional coverage as well, such as "medigap" coverage, policies designed to provide people on Medicare with supplemental payments. The medigap policies cover some of the expenses that Medicare does not, including some of the deductibles.

As required by federal legislation effective in 1992, state insurance commissioners have designed 10 standard medigap policies that may be marketed, offering a range of benefits from basic to comprehensive. The core benefits included in each policy include payment of the patient's 20 percent share of physician fees, payment of the patient's $157-per-day portion of hospital bills for the third month of hospitalization (Medicare covers the first 60 days), and limited coverage for subsequent hospitalization. More comprehensive coverage available in various of the other plans includes the $658 annual hospital deductible, the $100 deductible for doctors' charges, doctor charges in excess of Medicare allowable costs, medical needs during foreign travel, eight weeks of nursing care at home, skilled nursing home services for days 21 through 100, and a variety of prescription drug benefits.

LONG-TERM CARE POLICIES

◇ Long-term care policies are meant to cover long-term nursing home stays, but most people who buy long-term care policies never collect anything, even if they enter a nursing home, because of deductibles, enforced waiting periods, and excluded services. Evaluate long-term care policies as you would a regular medical insurance policy, by outlining a typical year of medical care and a worst-case scenario, and see how much of the expense you would bear and how much would be paid by the insurance company. (See *Consumer Reports* Ratings in June 1991 issue.)

Assess the probability that you will need nursing home care realistically, and consider your insurance accordingly. Remember that certain home health care and hospice care are included in Medicare coverage. If your family's elderly members have remained healthy and needed some assistance but not full-time care, chances are you may not need a long-term care policy. Even if your family history contains many illnesses that required long hospital stays, a long-term care policy may still not be right for you. Long-term care policies are still a relatively new phenomenon and they are aggressively marketed. Make sure you investigate with special care. Unless your income and assets are substantial, your money will be better spent in expanding your current medical insurance.

HOUSING AFTER RETIREMENT

As you mature, you must decide where to live. If your house is paid for and you are surrounded by old friends and family, you may decide to continue living in the house where you lived with your family. Many people, however, find that having a great deal of equity tied up in their home is a luxury they cannot afford. For others whose homes are not yet paid for, the combination of mortgage payments, property taxes, insurance, and upkeep is simply unmanageable. If you are in either of these categories, consider the alternatives, such as a condominium, a retirement community, or an apartment. With these options you will cut your expenses and management obligations and will free at least some equity in your home for investing.

The once-in-a-lifetime exclusion at age 55 of $125,000 of profit from the sale of your house will substantially reduce your tax cost if you decide to sell your home and scale down. But if you have considerably more profit in your home, you may want to retain it until your death; when you die, the house would receive a new tax basis equal to its fair market value, so your survivors could sell it with no income tax consequences.

Your home is one of your biggest assets. If you need to derive cash from your house, there are several ways to do it. The most obvious is to sell the house and move out, but while you will end up with a lump sum of cash, you may owe taxes on some or all of that money. And you will then have to purchase a new place to live, assuming that you can locate the kind of mortgage payments that fit your budget.

Another solution is to sell your house and lease it back, an arrangement that has worked quite successfully between many parents and their grown children in situations where the parents need cash and the children need a practical investment.

If you are at least 62 years old and you have considerable equity in your home, a reverse mortgage may work for you, whereby you take the loan proceeds in monthly installments and they are repaid from your estate. The monthly payment you receive is tax-free, since it is a loan rather than income.

If you plan to live in your house for as long as you are able, and if you don't wish to leave it to heirs, you can donate it to charity in exchange for the right to live in the house for the rest of your life. In this way you will reduce estate taxes and administration costs at the time of your death, and you will receive a current income tax deduction for the value of your gift.

ESTATE PLANNING

When you die, your estate gathers together all of your property, pays your legal debts, pays estate taxes and administrative expenses, and distributes the rest of your property to your heirs. Of course, your estate cannot do this on its own. (See chapter 6.)

If you would like to make certain that when you die your property goes to those whom you wish to have it, and that the least amount is spent on administration costs and estate taxes, then you need a will. Your will is a part of your overall estate plan, which is a study of your entire situation to ensure that your last wishes will be carried out at the least cost to your estate and your heirs.

In your will you will appoint an executor to be in charge, but if you die without a will the probate court of your state takes over. It is the function of the probate court to see that the laws of your state are carried out, and that the property is distributed to the heirs designated under state law, usually a surviving spouse and children. If you have no husband or children, state law dictates the succession of distribution to other family members.

If you die intestate, i.e., without a will, you are ensuring that the administration of your estate will be as costly as possible, since the courts will have to appoint professionals to carry out the law, and those professionals will have to be paid.

The Will Your State Provides for You

◇ Depending upon the state in which you reside, here is the will your state provides for you if you fail to write your own:

Being of sound mind, I declare this to be my last will and testament.

FIRST, I give to my children two-thirds of all my property, and to my husband what is left. It is his duty to support the children out of his share.

SECOND, I appoint my husband as guardian of my children, but as a safeguard, he shall report to the Probate Court each year and give an accounting of how he spent the children's money. As a further safeguard, my husband must purchase a performance bond to guarantee that he uses proper judgment in handling, investing, and spending my children's money.

THIRD, if my husband is not living at the time of my death and my children are minors, I direct the Probate Court to select a guardian for my children. If the Court wishes, it may appoint a stranger.

FOURTH, I direct that no effort be made to lower taxes or administrative fees, since I prefer to have my money used for governmental purposes rather than for the benefit of my husband and children.

IN WITNESS WHEREOF, I now proclaim this to be my last will.

CONSTRUCTING A WILL

◇ There are many ways in which you can leave your property to others:

1. You can make an outright gift while you are alive, with no strings attached.
2. You can put property into joint tenancy, which means that although you continue to control the property while you are alive, it will automatically pass to the surviving joint tenant when you die.
3. You can put property in trust for someone, with you or someone else as trustee. The terms of the trust agreement you write will dictate to whom and when the property is distributed. There are two basic types of trusts: irrevocable and living (revocable). Once you establish an irrevocable trust and place property into it, you may not change the terms of the trust, terminate the trust, or withdraw the property, other than through distributions called for in the trust instrument. A revocable living trust, on the other hand, allows you to make changes to the terms of the trust and add or withdraw property at any time during your lifetime. At your death, the living trust becomes irrevocable and cannot be changed. Both types of trusts avoid probate, and the irrevocable trust, depending on its terms, may remove assets from your taxable

estate and also reduce your income taxes, since income will be taxed to the trust itself or to its beneficiaries on income they derive from the trust.

4. Your will can be the vehicle that distributes everything else, either by specific bequest or by granting a life estate to an heir, with the balance going to someone else or to a charity. In your will, you will also appoint an executor for your estate, and you will usually dictate that the executor serve without costly bond.

In most states, you can draw up your own will if you do it in the proper format with the proper witnessing. But be careful: If you do not follow the rules exactly, your will could be declared invalid or become the subject of a costly battle among your heirs. If possible, your will should be prepared by a professional to prevent any disputes.

Your will also can protect your minor children. In the will, you can designate who will take physical and financial custody of your children. The physical and financial guardians do not have to be the same person. For example, you may wish to appoint your brother and his wife to be the guardians of your children in case of your death, but designate your financial adviser to be their financial guardian. If you are divorced at the time of your death and your children's father would become their physical guardian as surviving parent, you may not want him to control the money from your estate. In this case, your will should specify that your assets pass to a testamentary trust for your children's benefit, to be administered by a trustee you designate.

If your child or another heir is handicapped, you must carefully plan your estate to take this into account. Many of the social service programs designed for the disabled are not available to those who have or receive assets or income above a maximum amount. If you leave property to a disabled or handicapped person outright or in trust, your heir may be disqualified from receiving those social services as a result. If other heirs are trustworthy, consider leaving money to them and asking them to use the money to care for your handicapped heir. For example, if one of your children is handicapped, you can leave additional money to one of your other children and ask the child to spend the additional money on the disabled sibling.

Your will should be reviewed on a regular basis, as well as upon the occurrence of major changes in circumstances:

1. Review your will if one of your heirs has died.
2. Review your will if you move to a different state, since laws differ from state to state.
3. Review your will if there is a change in the economics or the health of your heirs. For example, a child who was previously doing well on her own may have suffered an accident and may now need special financial help.
4. Review your will if your assets or debts have increased or decreased substantially. You may decide to add or delete heirs, or to leave property to charity to save estate taxes.
5. Amend your will if the executor you named has died or become incapacitated, or if the guardian you named for your children will not be able to serve.
6. Review your will each time there is a substantial change in the law.

In some states, such as California, probate and administration expenses are very high. These expenses are charged as a percentage of the property that passes to your heirs, either as the result of your will or by way of state law if you have no will. Establishing a living trust reduces these expenses, since such a trust limits the amount that passes either through your will or through the laws of intestacy. Any property that you put in trust will pass on your death in accordance with the terms of your living trust agreement. Since that property is not administered by the probate court, the probate and administrative expenses will be saved, which will pass more money to your heirs. With a living trust, you can make the same bequests and devises that you would in your will, so long as property to be governed by the trust is titled in the name of yourself as trustee. Do not attempt to draw up your own trust agreement. Remember, you are skirting the probate courts, and you want to make sure that you do so in precisely the proper legal form. Money expended now for a properly constructed living trust will save a great deal of administrative expenses in the future.

The estate tax structure is such that every dollar over $600,000 is taxed at 37 to 55 percent, resulting in a large amount that must go to the government rather than to your heirs. To compute the value of your estate, add the value of your assets less your outstanding debts, the face value of life insurance policies on which you are both owner and insured, and the cash value of any policies on someone else's life on which you are named owner. If you have made annual gifts in excess of $10,000 per beneficiary, you must add those excess taxable gifts to your estate as well. From this amount, subtract estimated funeral and administrative expenses, which will probably range between 5 and 10 percent of your gross estate. Now subtract the amount you may be leaving to your husband or to charity, and that is the amount of your taxable estate. If your taxable estate exceeds $600,000, the excess will be taxed at graduated rates that start at 37 percent and rapidly increase to 55 percent. The state in which you live may also levy an estate or inheritance tax, but all or a portion of that tax may be deductible from the federal estate tax. If your taxable estate will exceed $600,000, your estate plan should include estate tax-saving devices, such as a gift-giving program, irrevocable insurance trusts, bypass testamentary trusts, and charitable trusts. These methods can save a substantial amount of taxes. If your estate is sizable, it is important for you to consult an estate attorney soon.

REDUCING ESTATE TAXES

◇ You can reduce estate taxes by shifting a portion of your assets to other family members. You may give up to $10,000 to anyone each year without incurring a gift tax. For example, if you have two children and five grandchildren, you may give them each up to $10,000 each year without paying tax. Through regular gift giving to a large group of beneficiaries, you can rapidly reduce your estate to the $600,000 level that is exempt from federal estate taxes. Regular gift giving is wise, and it is gratifying to see your family enjoy your largesse while you are alive, but take care not to deplete your estate below the amount you need to ensure a comfortable future.

Another way to pass wealth to others is by using your investment expertise and capital to build wealth in their names rather than in yours. For example, rather than investing $10,000 in a mutual fund in your name and watching it grow to $20,000 in five years, invest the money in your beneficiary's name instead. In that way, your beneficiary's estate will grow rather than yours, reducing the taxes on your estate when you die.

If estate taxes will be high, you may wish to purchase a life insurance policy that will pay those taxes when you die. Since the proceeds from life insurance policies that you own are a part of your estate, you could be compounding your estate tax problems. If you plan to fund future estate taxes with insurance, create an irrevocable life insurance trust in the name of which the insurance policies will be purchased and owned. You may then make monetary gifts to the trust each year to pay the premiums as they come due. You can also transfer existing policies to the trust, but the proceeds will be part of your taxable estate if you die within three years of the transfer.

If you have a favorite charity and wish to leave a portion of your estate to it when you die, consider making a gift to the charity while you are alive rather than at your death, to secure a current income tax deduction and reduce your taxable estate. If you wish to make a gift to charity and yet do not want to diminish your estate, purchase a life insurance policy that will pay your heirs an amount equivalent to your gift to charity. If the life insurance policy is purchased in the names of your heirs or an irrevocable life insurance trust, it will not be a part of your estate when you die, and you can make annual gifts to your heirs so that they can pay the premiums.

Appendixes:
WORKSHEETS

Appendix A
GOALS WORKSHEET

	HOW IMPORTANT? (0–5)	WHEN?	HOW MUCH IN TODAY'S DOLLARS?
Pay off credit cards	_____	_____	_____
Create a cash reserve	_____	_____	_____
Buy a new car	_____	_____	_____
Educate children	_____	_____	_____
Go back to school	_____	_____	_____
Take a sabbatical	_____	_____	_____
Buy a luxury item	_____	_____	_____
Make a down payment for a new home	_____	_____	_____
Travel or take a vacation	_____	_____	_____
Finance a new business	_____	_____	_____
Retire early	_____	_____	_____
Purchase a vacation home	_____	_____	_____
Invest in an IRA	_____	_____	_____
Establish an emergency fund	_____	_____	_____
Buy a new wardrobe	_____	_____	_____
Other _____	_____	_____	_____
Other _____	_____	_____	_____

Appendix B

REACHING YOUR FINANCIAL OBJECTIVES WORKSHEET

1. Goal _____
2. How much do I need in today's dollars? _____
3. For how many years do I have to save? _____
4. How much must I save each month? _____
   (Divide today's cost by the number from the table below.)
5. How will I save for my goal? _____
   (From current earnings, raises, gifts, inheritances, etc.)
6. How will I invest these savings? _____
   (For example, children's education might be funded through investment in zero-coupon or U.S. Savings Bonds, both of which are purchased at a discount and pay no interest until maturity; a home
   purchase might be funded through growth stocks; retirement income
   might be funded through a fixed annuity, etc.)

YEARS TO GOAL	FACTOR
1	12
2	25
3	39
4	54
5	70
10	164
15	291
20	462
25	693
30	1005

Appendix C
ESTABLISHING YOUR CURRENT
FINANCIAL POSITION WORKSHEET

Assets	CURRENT VALUE	COULD BE CONVERTED TO CASH	INCOME AVAILABLE
CASH ACCOUNTS			
_____	_____	_____	_____
_____	_____	_____	_____
_____	_____	_____	_____
STOCKS AND BONDS			
_____	_____	_____	_____
_____	_____	_____	_____
_____	_____	_____	_____
NOTES RECEIVABLE FROM REAL ESTATE CONTRACTS, PERSONAL LOANS, ETC.			
_____	_____	_____	_____
_____	_____	_____	_____
_____	_____	_____	_____
RETIREMENT ASSETS			
_____	_____	_____	_____
_____	_____	_____	_____
_____	_____	_____	_____
LIFE INSURANCE			
_____	_____	_____	_____
_____	_____	_____	_____
_____	_____	_____	_____
REAL ESTATE			
_____	_____	_____	_____
_____	_____	_____	_____
_____	_____	_____	_____

Assets	CURRENT VALUE	COULD BE CONVERTED TO CASH	INCOME AVAILABLE
BUSINESS ASSETS			
PERSONAL PROPERTY			
TOTAL ASSETS			

Liabilities

NOTES AND MORTGAGES PAYABLE			
CREDIT CARD BALANCES			
OTHER DEBTS			
TOTAL LIABILITIES			
NET WORTH			

Appendix D
CALCULATING YOUR LIFE INSURANCE NEEDS WORKSHEET

IMMEDIATE CASH NEEDS IF YOU SHOULD DIE TOMORROW
1. Cash available _____
2. Assets that could be sold _____
3. Total (1 + 2) _____
Subtract:
4. Debts to be paid off immediately _____
5. Funeral and death costs _____
6. Amount remaining (3 − 4 − 5); if
   negative, must be covered by insurance _____

EDUCATION FUND FOR CHILDREN IF YOU DIE
1. Total cost of college in today's dollars _____
2. Number of children _____
3. Total college costs (1 × 2) (assuming
   inflation equals after-tax investment
   return) _____
Subtract funding from existing sources:
4. College fund already established _____
5. Scholarships and loans _____
6. Other (grandparents, earnings) _____
7. Additional college fund needed (3 − 4
   − 5 − 6); this amount must be covered
   by insurance _____

SPOUSE'S LIVING EXPENSES UNTIL RETIREMENT
1. Annual income needs (75 percent of
   current income) _____
Subtract:
2. Annual earnings of spouse _____
3. Other annual income and benefits _____
4. Supplemental annual income needed (1
   − 2 − 3) _____
5. Times number of years until retirement × _____

6. Total supplemental annual income
   needed (4 × 5)   _____

7. Times growth-inflation factor:

Less than 5 years	.95	
Up to 10 years	.90	
Up to 20 years	.85	× _____
Up to 30 years	.80	factor
More than 30 years	.75	

8. Living expense fund needed (6 × 7)—
   must be covered by insurance   ==========

SPOUSE'S RETIREMENT NEEDS

1. Annual income needs (75 percent of
   current income)   _____

Subtract:

2. Annual Social Security benefits
   expected (complete Form 7004 and
   submit to Social Security
   Administration to obtain this
   information, or estimate based on the
   following figures: average benefits =
   $9,800; maximum benefits = $14,700)   _____

3. Annual pension benefits   _____

4. Retirement income needed, in today's
   dollars (1 − 2 − 3)   _____

5. Times retirement income factor   × 22

6. Amount needed at retirement (age 65)
   (4 × 5)   _____

7. Times years-to-retirement factor:

Less than 5 years	.95	
Up to 10 years	.85	
Up to 20 years	.75	× _____
Up to 30 years	.60	factor
More than 30 years	.55	

8. Amount needed to fund retirement
   (6 × 7)   _____

9. Amounts now available for retirement   _____

10. Additional amount needed to fund retirement (8 − 9), which must be covered by insurance   ═══════

TOTAL LIFE INSURANCE NEEDED
1. Immediate cash needs if you should die   ─────────
2. Education fund for children if you die   ─────────
3. Spouse's living expenses until retirement   ─────────
4. Spouse's retirement needs   ─────────
5. Total life insurance needed (1 + 2 + 3 + 4)   ─────────
6. Total life insurance owned   ─────────
7. Additional insurance needed (5 − 6)   ═══════

Appendix E
ANALYZING YOUR INVESTMENTS WORKSHEET

INVESTMENT ASSETS

    For each investment asset listed in Appendix C, supply the following information:

1. Asset _____
2. Invested for safety, tax benefits, appreciation, or yield? _____
3. Current value _____
4. Expected annual appreciation percentage _____
5. Expected annual yield percentage _____
6. Total expected return (4 + 5) _____
7. Safety factor (1 = relatively safe; 5 = very risky)

Now compile the information below:

	1 CURRENT VALUE	2 TOTAL RETURN PERCENTAGE	3 SAFETY FACTOR	4 COL 1 × COL 2	5 COL 1 × COL 3
Asset 1	_____	_____	_____	_____	_____
Asset 2	_____	_____	_____	_____	_____
Asset 3	_____	_____	_____	_____	_____
Asset 4	_____	_____	_____	_____	_____
etc.					
Total	_____	_____	_____	_____	_____

Portfolio total return (⁴⁄₁) _____
Portfolio safety factor (⁵⁄₁) _____

RETIREMENT PLANS
Name of plan _____
Name and address of administrator _____
_____
Current value of fund _____
Payout terms _____
Survivor benefits _____

Location of documents regarding plan _____

_____

LIFE INSURANCE
Company name and address _____

_____

Policy number _____ Type _____
Amount _____ Date of policy _____
Beneficiary _____
Payout terms _____
Location of policy _____

Appendix F
DETERMINING WHEN TO SELL ASSETS WORKSHEET

For each investment asset listed in Appendix C, supply the following information:

Asset _____

When do you estimate this asset should be sold? _____

What criteria will indicate the right time to sell? _____
_____

Special steps to be taken in the next year or two (refinancing, improvements, etc.) _____
_____

Appendix G
ASSESSING YOUR REQUIRED MANAGEMENT SKILLS WORKSHEET

Here are the steps to take in evaluating the nature of the management skills needed to supervise each of your investments:

1.   What are the specific management requirements for the investment?

_____

2.   If the asset is to be sold once your spouse dies, what steps must be taken to sell it?

_____

_____

3.   If the asset is to be kept after your spouse's death, what skills will be required to maintain and supervise it?

_____

_____

4. · If you lack the requisite management skills, list those you will need to acquire and how you plan to attain them.

_____

_____

5.   If either you or your spouse is involved in a lawsuit, review the progress of the lawsuit, the expected outcome, and the procedure that the other spouse should follow upon the death of the person named in the suit.

_____

_____

Appendix H
KEY ADVISERS
WORKSHEET

Make a list of your key advisers, with their addresses and phone numbers. Update it regularly.

Accountant _____ Phone _____
 Address _____
Attorney _____ Phone _____
 Address _____
Stockbroker _____ Phone _____
 Address _____
Financial Adviser _____ Phone _____
 Address _____
Insurance Agent _____ Phone _____
 Address _____
Banker _____ Phone _____
 Address _____
Executor of Your Will _____ Phone _____
 Address _____
Other Adviser _____ Phone _____
 Address _____
Other Adviser _____ Phone _____
 Address _____

Appendix I
MAKING FUNERAL ARRANGEMENTS WORKSHEET

Use this worksheet to keep a record of the funeral arrangements, if any, which you and your spouse have specified. Designate the clergy or other service conductor you might wish to officiate, where the service should be held, specific information regarding burial or cremation, including cemetery plot, mausoleum entombment, urn burial, urn in niche, or scattering of remains, donation of body or body organs, type of coffin and price range, coffin to be open or closed, service to be open to public, for relatives and friends, or just immediate family, special wishes regarding speakers, music, readings, etc., and charities for memorial contributions.

Clergy or other to officiate _____

Location and nature of service _____

Interment, cremation, burial at _____

Information re cemetery plot
or memorial society _____

Special wishes for funeral (casket, viewing, music, readings, clothing, flowers) _____

_____

Charities for memorial contributions _____

PALLBEARERS
Name _____ Phone _____
    Address _____
Name _____ Phone _____
    Address _____
Name _____ Phone _____
    Address _____
Name _____ Phone _____
    Address _____
Name _____ Phone _____
    Address _____
Name _____ Phone _____
    Address _____

PEOPLE TO NOTIFY OF DEATH

Name _____ Phone _____
    Address _____

Name _____ Phone _____
    Address _____

Name _____ Phone _____
    Address _____

Name _____ Phone _____
    Address _____

Name _____ Phone _____
    Address _____

Name _____ Phone _____
    Address _____

Name _____ Phone _____
    Address _____

Name _____ Phone _____
    Address _____

Appendix J
FINANCIAL EDUCATION PROGRAM WORKSHEET

1. Review the management skills listed in Appendix G. Identify courses, seminars, and reading material that will increase these skills.

_____

_____

2. Discuss other kinds of financial education that would benefit you, and list the specifics of a program that will give you the ability to manage your finances more effectively and with greater confidence.

_____

_____

3. Make a list of follow-up sessions to cover those steps not completed in this contingency-day session.

_____

_____

4. Schedule further follow-up sessions as needed, and schedule a date in one year for your annual contingency-day discussion, as follows:

_____

_____

Recommended Reading

2 ON YOUR OWN

BAILARD, BIEHL & KAISER, INC. *How to Buy the Right Insurance at the Right Price*. Homewood, Ill.: Dow Jones–Irwin, 1989.

BREITBARD, STANLEY H., AND CARPENTER, DONNA S. *Price Waterhouse Book of Personal Financial Planning*. New York: Henry Holt, 1990.

BROWN, CHARLENE. *The Consumer's Credit Book: How to Repair or Get Credit*. Irvine, Calif.: United Resource Books, 1991.

BRUNETTE, WILLIAM K. *Conquer Your Debt: How To Solve Your Credit Problems*. Englewood Cliffs, N.J.: Prentice-Hall, 1990.

CARD, EMILY. *The Ms. Money Book: Strategies for Prospering in the Coming Decade*. New York: E. P. Dutton, 1990.

ESANU, WARREN H., DICKMAN, BARRY, ZUCKERMAN, ELIAS M., AND POLLET, MICHAEL N. *Guide to Income Tax Preparation*. Yonkers, N.Y.: Consumer Reports Books, 1991.

SAVAGE, TERRY. *Terry Savage Talks Money: The Common-Sense Guide to Money Matters*. Chicago: Longman Financial, 1990.

3 SHARING YOUR LIFE

DENNIS, MARGUERITE J. *Keys to Financing a College Education*. New York: Barron, 1990.

FELTON-COLLINS, VICTORIA, WITH BROWN, SUZANNE BLAIR. *Couples & Money*. New York: Bantam Books, 1990.

SALTMAN, DAVID, AND SCHAFFNER, HARRY. *Don't Get Married Until You Read This: A Layman's Guide to Prenuptial Agreements*. New York: Barron, 1989.

4   INVESTING FOR YOUR FUTURE

BAMFORD, JANET, BLYSKAL, JEFF, CARD, EMILY, AND JACOBSON, AILEEN. *Complete Guide to Managing Your Money*. Yonkers, N.Y.: Consumer Reports Books, 1989.

KANTOR, SANFORD S., J.D., AND BERNSTEIN, JOEL H., J.D., WITH KENNEDY, DAVID W., AND THE EDITORS OF CONSUMER REPORTS BOOKS. *Stand Up to Your Stockbroker*. Yonkers, N.Y.: Consumer Reports Books, 1991.

KLOTT, GARRY. *The Complete Financial Guide to the 1990s*. New York: Random House, 1990.

PORTER, SYLVIA. *Sylvia Porter's Your Finances in the 1990s*. Englewood Cliffs, N.J.: Prentice-Hall, 1990.

THOMSETT, MICHAEL C., AND THE EDITORS OF CONSUMER REPORTS BOOKS . *How to Buy a House, Condo, or Co-op*. Yonkers, N.Y.: Consumer Reports Books, 1990.

5   DIVORCE

AGRAN, LIBBIE. *The Economics of Divorce: A Financial Survival Kit for Women*. Pasadena, Calif.: Trilogy Books, 1990.

BRENNER, LOIS, AND STEIN, ROBERT. *Getting Your Share: A Woman's Guide to Successful Divorce Strategies*. New York: Crown Publishers, 1989.

CROUCH, HOLMES F. *All Year Tax Guide: Going Through Divorce*. San Marcos, Calif.: R. J. Erdmann, 1990.

FELTON-COLLINS, VICTORIA, WOODHOUSE, VIOLET, AND BLAKEMAN, M.C. *Divorce and Money*. Berkeley, Calif.: Nolo Press, 1991.

ROBERTSON, CHRISTINA. *A Woman's Guide to Divorce and Decision Making*. New York: Simon & Schuster, 1989.

6   WIDOWHOOD

CAINE, LYNN. *Being a Widow*. New York: Penguin, 1990.

GATES, PHILOMENE. *Suddenly Alone: A Woman's Guide to Widowhood*. New York: Harper & Row, 1990.

RICE, REBECCA. *A Time to Mourn: One Woman's Journey Through Widowhood*. New York: New American Library, 1990.

EDITORS OF CONSUMER REPORTS BOOKS. *Funerals: Consumers' Last Rights*. Mount Vernon, N.Y.: Consumer Reports Books, 1977.

7   ON YOUR OWN AGAIN

BOLLES, RICHARD N. *What Color Is Your Parachute?* Berkeley, Calif.: Ten Speed Press, 1991.

DANNA, JO. *Starting Over: You in the New Workplace*. Briarwood, N.Y.: Palomino Press, 1990.

DUDLEY, DENISE. *Every Woman's Guide to Career Success*. Mission, Kan.: Skill Path Publishers, 1989.

LESTER, MARY. *A Woman's Guide to Starting a Small Business*. Babylon, N.Y.: Pilot Books, 1989.

LOWNES, MILLICENT G. *The Purple Rose Within: A Woman's Basic Guide for Developing a Business Plan*. Nashville, Tenn.: Business of Your Own, 1989.

ZUCKERMAN, LAURIE B. *On Your Own: A Woman's Guide to Building a Business*. Dover, N.H.: Upstart Publishers, 1990.

8   RETIREMENT

BELEN, DAVID W. *Creative Estate Planning for the 1990s: A Guide for Middle- & Upper-Income Americans*. New York: Macmillan, 1991.

HARDY, C. COLBURN. *Retire Prosperously*. Englewood Cliffs, N.J.: Prentice-Hall, 1990.

HANSEN, LEONARD J. *Life Begins at 50*. New York: Barron, 1989.

OSHIRO, CARL, SNYDER, HARRY, AND THE EDITORS OF CONSUMER REPORTS BOOKS. *Medicare/Medigap*. Yonkers, N.Y.: Consumer Reports Books, 1989.

Index